Ed Sheeran

A+ The Unauthorised Biography

Ed Sheeran

A+ The Unauthorised Biography

David Nolan

JOHN BLAKE

Published by John Blake Publishing Ltd,
3 Bramber Court, 2 Bramber Road,
London W14 9PB, England

www.johnblakepublishing.co.uk

www.facebook.com/Johnblakepub facebook
twitter.com/johnblakepub twitter

First published in hardback in 2012

ISBN: 9781782190202

British Library Cataloguing-in-Publication Data:

A catalogue record for this book is available from the British Library.

Design by www.envydesign.co.uk

Printed and bound in Great Britain
by CPI Group (UK) Ltd

1 3 5 7 9 10 8 6 4 2

Papers used by John Blake Publishing are natural, recyclable
products made from wood grown in sustainable forests.
The manufacturing processes conform to the environmental
regulations of the country of origin.

For Malcolm Fraser, 1939 – 2012.
A real mentor.

CONTENTS

ABOUT THE
AUTHOR

David Nolan has written for newspapers, magazines, radio and television. He has authored music biographies on Tony Wilson of Factory Records, Damon Albarn of Blur, New Order's Bernard Sumner and Simon Cowell. He's also made television documentaries on The Smiths, Echo and the Bunnymen and the Sex Pistols.

ACKNOWLEDGEMENTS

Many thanks to Gordon Burns, Joe Doran, Gary Dunne, Richard Hanley and Colin Hirst of Thomas Mills High School, Framlingham; Lizi Hanley, Tony Moore at The Bedford in Balham and Jonathan De Veaux from The Savoy Entertainment Centre in Inglewood, Los Angeles. Thanks also to editor Lucian Randall, Ian Cranna and Rosie Virgo at John Blake Publishing.

INTRODUCTION

It's 4 June 2012 and a musical party is underway in London. It's being staged to mark the Queen's Diamond Jubilee and a host of stars from the worlds of pop, rock and classical musical are gearing up to perform to a worldwide audience.

As they do, a pattern begins to emerge: all the acts seem to be doing their best to outdo each other to catch the audience's collective eye. On a specially constructed stage around the Victoria Memorial fountain outside Buckingham Palace, Aston from JLS does a back somersault, Grace Jones sings and hula hoops at the same time all the way through her best known song 'Slave to the Rhythm' and Gary Barlow and Cheryl Cole take Lady Antebellum's 'Need You Now' round the back of the fountain and murder it.

Among the bombast and the nonsense, one performance stands out – largely because of the performer's singular failure to try to *make it* stand out. In front of an invited audience of 20,000 people, a special area packed with members of the royal family and VIPs, a quarter of a million members of the public stretching away into the distance down The Mall and a worldwide TV audience, a young man with an undersized guitar sings a song about a crack-addicted prostitute. His guitar has a picture of a paw print on the front and someone has written a name on it in felt tip: Nigel. Just before he went on stage Nigel's 21-year-old owner tweeted a message to his fans: 'so apparently 1 billion people are tuning in tonight. no pressure then'.

The young singer had only signed a record deal the previous year, yet here he was sharing a stage with the likes of Sir Elton John, Sir Tom Jones and Sir Paul McCartney. The performer's first instinct when he came off stage was to communicate with his fans: 'Well that was fun!' he said via Twitter.

From sofa-surfer to superstar, Ed Sheeran has come a long way in what appears to be a very short time. He's made it look easy. It hasn't been. 'I was a hard sell for the major labels,' he says of the years he gigged relentlessly to slowly build a devoted audience. 'Here's a ginger kid who raps with a guitar. That's not a good start.'

ONE

SO HEBDEN BRIDGE

'I remember big hills,' Ed Sheeran says when
recalling his West Yorkshire childhood. 'I know
I lived at the top of one.'

The area of West Yorkshire where Ed Sheeran is from is
known as Calderdale. Tucked to the east of the
Pennines, Calderdale is very proud of the young man born
there on 17 February 1991. The local paper likes to refer to
Sheeran as the 'Calderdale Singer-Songwriter'.

If Calderdale were a song type it would be a mash-up. It's
a series of contrasts that sit side by side: the tea shop and
the tower block; the brass band and boutique hotel; the
Mosque and the Mecca Bingo Hall. It's independent and
likes to wear its independence proudly on its collective
sleeve. But there's one part of Calderdale that doesn't just

display its independence – it screams it from the rooftops. It's the part of Calderdale where Ed Sheeran began his life: Hebden Bridge.

As you drive into Hebden Bridge from nearby Halifax, a roadside sign states that the town lays claim to '500 Years of Creativity'. As you drive out, the reverse sign tells you that you are leaving by camply proclaiming: 'That was *so* Hebden Bridge'.

It is home to artists, hippies, TV producers and seekers of alternative lifestyles. It's also the 'most lesbian' town in Britain, with more same-sex female couples than anywhere else. But Hebden Bridge is very aware of its image and reputation and isn't averse to sending itself up now and again – there's even a furnishings shop called 'Home...Oh!'

The groups of creative and alternative incomers that descended on the area in the 1970s saved a declining mill town and turned it into their own little slice of Bohemia. Hebden Bridge is Bohemian simply because the people who moved there decided they wanted it to be that way. The creative enclave is a base for many people working in Manchester, Leeds and Halifax because of its central location and handy train links. The charming late 19th-century train station that serves the town obviously made an impression on the young Ed: 'I remember being four and wanting to a train driver – that was the only thing that interested me,' he told KidsofGrime TV. Not that he's entirely given up on the idea: 'I'll become a train driver one day.'

Ed's parents, London-born John Sheeran and Imogen

Lock, could be said to fit the Hebden Bridge profile pretty well. Both are passionate about the arts: John as an art lecturer and curator, Imogen as a promoter of the arts through her work as a PR consultant to the creative industries. 'His mum was very much into PR,' says Gordon Burns, Ed's cousin. Burns is a radio and TV presenter, best known as the face of *The Krypton Factor*. 'His dad used to run these art galleries – he's very deep into the arts – John Sheeran's a nice, easy-going guy. All the Sheerans are like that, incredibly laid back. That comes all the way down through the family – easy-going, fun and gentle – and Ed seems to have it as well. Nothing fazes him, his feet are firmly on the ground, he knows what he's doing. Which is what I'd expect of a Sheeran.'

Imogen Sheeran's creativity would also come out through her love of making jewellery. Today, her handmade items are proudly sold at Hebden Bridge's Earth Spirit shop on Market Street. The shop's owner Catrina Gledhill is keen to flag up Ed's local connection, especially as the jewellery designs are intrinsically linked to Ed's childhood: 'Ed grew up in Hebden Bridge so it's great that Ed's talented mum, Imogen, has chosen to supply a local business,' she told the *Hebden Bridge Times*. 'Many of the items from the collection are based on his favourite sweets, such as Liquorice Allsorts and Smarties or on Ed's song lyrics.'

The Sheerans loved the town so much they didn't let the fact that their work regularly took them to London and Manchester put them off living there. For John, it was as curator of the Dulwich Picture Gallery in southeast London.

For Imogen it was as a media consultant for the National Portrait Gallery in the capital and then, nearer to home, working for Manchester Galleries just over the Pennines.

Their first son Matthew was born in 1989. Perhaps aware of the changes their lives would undergo after starting a family, John and Imogen left their jobs and set up an arts consultancy business together in 1990. Ed – known when he was young as Teddy – was born a year later. They still went where the work took them, usually London. Most weekends would be spent travelling to and from the capital with their two young sons in tow. The Sheerans would play music in the car to while away the time on the long journeys. 'Basically, my parents had to commute and I'd go with them,' Ed later explained to *Q* magazine. 'It'd be the same albums over and over again – Dylan's *The Times They Are A-Changin'*, Clapton's *Unplugged*, Joni Mitchell's *Blue*. Now, listening back to all that stuff, it just reminds me of homely, warm stuff. It's really cool.'

The trips were so regular – and the album choices so consistent – that Ed began to learn the words and eventually he started to sing along. The albums on the Sheerans' car stereo may have spanned a 30-year period, from 1964 (Bob Dylan) to 1992 (Clapton's *Unplugged*), but they all clearly share a gentle, acoustic vibe that would make a clear impression on Ed, as would the more traditional aspects of Irish folk music: 'The first album that introduced me to music was Van Morrison's *Irish Heartbeat* with Irish traditional group The Chieftans,' he later told *On Stage*. 'The first music I heard was trad music. That was a major influence. There was an Irish folk band called Planxty that I was brought up on.'

John Sheeran's musical tastes seemed to dominate and his acoustic and traditional choices would prove to have a lasting effect on Ed. But anything overly rock 'n' roll was frowned upon in the Sheeran household. 'My dad's never been into rock music – ever,' Ed told *The Age* newspaper in Australia in 2012. 'We've never had a Queen CD in the house.'

Motown seems to have been as up-tempo as things got chez Sheeran and Stevie Wonder – who Ed would perform with in 2012 at the Queen's Diamond Jubilee Concert – was a particular favourite: 'My dad had [Wonder's 1974 album] *Fulfillingness' First Finale* on record,' Ed later told *The Guardian*. 'That was the first Stevie album I heard and there was a track called "They Won't Go When I Go", and that's been one of my favourite songs ever since. He's just great.'

Music producer Jake Gosling, who worked with Ed on his early EPs and later the + album, believes that Sheeran's upbringing was key to his later life as a musician: 'He's from a very creative background, his Mum and Dad have supported him all the way,' he later wrote on his blog. 'He was brought up surrounded by artists, painting, sculpture and the obscure. For any growing mind this set a light. Ed uses his music to communicate what he really feels and speaks from the heart.'

The creative, musical atmosphere within the family clearly had an effect on both boys: Ed's brother Matthew would go on to study music at university and is now an award-winning classical composer, having received a young composer's award at the annual Presteigne Festival in 2010 and a composition award at the international Shipley Arts Festival the same year. Ed and Matthew look like twins – both have the flaming red Sheeran hair and both share the same sharp facial features.

As a young child, Ed's features would cause him issues, some of them continuing into his teens. He had what he would later describe as a 'massive' birthmark on his face removed by undergoing laser surgery. He would later claim that having the birthmark led to him developing a speech impediment. 'When I was younger I had a really bad stutter and had to do a lot of speech therapy,' he revealed to *The Sun* in 2011. 'I overcame it when I was about 13 or 14 years old. I still have a bit of a stutter when I get excited but it's not as bad as it was.'

The birthmark and the stutter – plus poor eyesight and hearing, not to mention his distinctive shock of red hair – seemed to have weighed heavily on the youngster. He would later describe his childhood as 'slightly depressing'. But it's hard to imagine a child being more nurtured and encouraged than he was. His was a deeply creative family environment – Ed would say an early ambition of his was to 'sort of paint and stuff' – and he even sent some of his early paintings into BBC kids' show *Blue Peter*.

Holidays for the Sheerans usually meant travelling to Ireland, where their family roots were strong. Ed's grandparents Bill and Ann had moved from London to County Wexford. Their marriage in the 1950s had caused a scandal in the family: Bill was a Protestant, Ann a Catholic. Ed would go and stay with his grandparents at their farm for the summer alongside other young members of his extended Irish family. Idyllic. His grandparents' farm was a playground for him and his young relatives. After a day spent running around collecting chickens' eggs, Ed would take a sleeping bag and camp out in the huge barn with his cousins – the Sheeran farm is still a retreat for Ed to this day. 'Ann, Ed's grandma, is gentle and laidback,' Gordon Burns told me. 'Bill, his granddad was a leading light in the British Boxing Board of Control and used to be an amateur boxer. Bill is an easygoing, laidback guy.'

The Irish connection also provided an upbringing steeped in the love and appreciation of music. In terms of his own involvement, Ed would join his mother singing in a choir at a very young age, the starting point for his love of song: 'It's just a love of mine that's been embedded into me since I was young – it was constant,' he later explained to the OTUmusic website.

To be nearer their work – and as it became time for Ed to start school – the Sheerans moved south to the beautiful Suffolk market town of Framlingham. By way of contrast to the groovy, hippy vibe of Hebden Bridge, Framlingham is steeped in history that makes the Calderdale town look like a newcomer. Dominated by its 12th-century castle, the town can trace its roots back to the Doomsday Book. Framlingham guards its history and beauty closely with a conservation area at the heart of the town designed to protect its charm. With a population of less than 3,000 it is as tasteful and well-appointed as anywhere in Britain and the town and its surrounding areas are very proud of Ed Sheeran – the local newspaper likes to refer to him as the 'Framlingham Singer-Songwriter'. Obviously. 'Growing up in Suffolk – because it's the countryside – it was very free and easy and relaxed,' was how Ed would later describe his new home.

Ed was enrolled into the Sir Robert Hitcham Primary School on College Road in Framlingham. The school describes itself as providing a 'happy and caring Christian learning environment, where individuality is celebrated, achievement nurtured, and every child empowered to reach their highest spiritual, educational, and personal potential.' It's the oldest primary school in Framlingham and is named after the former owner of Framlingham Castle.

John and Imogen Sheeran continued with their art consultancy, but having creatively-minded parents wasn't always appreciated by young Ed. 'I remember during the yoyo craze my mum wouldn't spend £8 and made me one out of jam jar lids and string. Can you imagine taking that to school? But now I see it was cool and I realise how amazing my parents are for not giving me that stuff – all the kids I knew with everything aren't really in a good place right now.'

Ed's love of singing was augmented by a gift from an uncle that was a little more eagerly received that his jam-jar-lid yoyo – a guitar. Ed would later become fascinated by the instrument after seeing Eric Clapton play at The Queen's Golden Jubilee concert in February 2002.

Clapton's performance also convinced Ed that he should concentrate on acoustic guitar: 'I used to be really into guitar-driven music,' Ed later told *Total Guitar* magazine, 'Guns N' Roses songs and stuff like that. I saw Clapton play "Layla" at the Golden Jubilee. That song is wicked.' Ed watched the event on television – Tom Jones, Sir Elton John and Sir Paul McCartney played as well. Ten years later, Ed Sheeran would play alongside them at the Queen's Diamond Jubilee concert.

There were a few guitar lessons to set him on the right path, but Ed mainly did it his way, taking a view that he seems to have stuck with: if a thing's worth doing, it's worth doing properly... and doing yourself. 'When I started playing guitar I was practising seven hours a day, just going through it,' he would later explain to OTUmusic. 'Friends would come round and say, Come out and I'd say, No I'm doing my music – I can't waste time. That actually happened.' A template for the future was already being set. Don't muck about. Do it properly. Work hard: 'Nothing is worth having unless it comes with hard work,' says Sheeran today.

He began to listen to more music from ever-widening sources. If it seems precocious to be doing this at such a young age ... that's because Ed Sheeran *was* precocious. His youth and enthusiasm began to combine with his eclectic tastes in music, plus the continuing influence of his parents' acoustic- based Hebden Bridge record collection. Van Morrison and Joni Mitchell albums nestled next to Elton John's *Greatest Hits* album and The Beatles in the Sheerans' record collection. Plus it's hard to imagine that their Framlingham home didn't have a reasonable collection of albums by John Martyn. The Anglo-Scots folk and jazz musician, who died in 2009, was notable for his use of the Echoplex tape delay effect, which allowed him to build up loops of sound and rhythm both live and in the studio. The technology Ed Sheeran would use in years to come was different, but the effect would be remarkably similar to the sound that Martyn produced. By way of contrast to Martyn's mellifluous soundscapes, Ed also professed a liking for punk and nu-metal, perhaps as a small act of rebellion against his family's mellower tastes: 'I was kind of brought up as a bit of a *Kerrang!* kid and when I was younger I loved bands like Blink 182, Offspring and Linkin Park,' he later confessed to *The Guardian*.

A cousin then introduced Ed to rap. Jethro Sheeran had already worked as a model and actor and must have seemed impossibly glamorous to young Ed. In 2002 Jethro was making inroads into a career in music. He had launched himself as a rap act under the slightly more street name of Alonestar, had acquired Simon Webbe of boyband Blue as a manager and was getting ready to tour with the likes of Blazin' Squad. Before he was 10 Ed Sheeran was listening to Jay-Z and Eminem. Then there was Tupac Shakur and The Notorious B.I.G. The gangster rappers were all across the news in the late 1990s after their violent deaths were attributed to rivalry between acts from the East and West coasts of America. The music and what it represented was as far removed from rural Suffolk as is possible, but the young Ed became enthralled. 'You might look at Eminem and Bob Dylan and say they're two totally different acts,' Ed told WatchMojo.com when asked about his diverse influences. 'But all you have to do with Eminem is put a guitar behind his words and it's a very similar thing. Folk music tells stories and hip hop tells stories. There's just a beat that separates it.'

In later years this hodgepodge of influences would baffle reviewers, who couldn't get a grip of Sheeran's music and its origins. He wasn't like other musicians because his frame of reference was different thanks to his age: 'I was born in '91 so most of my musical growing up was done from 2000 onwards,' he later explained to the *Daily Telegraph*. 'If I'd been born in the 1980s most of my musical growing up would have been through the Blur and Oasis period so I would have been a hardcore indie fan.'

Though still very young, Sheeran seems to have received a surprising amount of leeway from his parents in terms of how he lived his life. This was to have a dramatic effect on him and his future when he was barely 11 years old. 'I've never really been a day person and I used to stay up at night and watch the music channels,' he later explained to *Q* magazine. 'This video came on at about four o'clock in the morning, just this dude's mouth singing and it turned out to be "Cannonball".'

The dude in the video was Damien Rice and seeing the 'Cannonball' video in the early hours of the morning would shape Sheeran's musical trajectory and change his life. The video, a bizarre collage of seemingly random images of scribbled words, toothbrushes and cats – with occasional glimpses of Rice's mouth – may have made an impression on Sheeran, but at the time it didn't make much of a dent in the charts. It would take several re-releases and two years before it would peak at Number 19 in the UK charts.

Irish singer-songwriter Rice was not necessarily the most obvious artist to connect with an 11-year-old boy, but there's a great deal about him that would directly inform Sheeran's later work. Rice's raw, emotional style, his confessional lyrics and stripped-down acoustic style would all feed into the Ed Sheeran we know today. Rice also possesses the ability to generate a communal live experience that appeals particularly to women – again, territory that Sheeran now occupies. The similarities continue: Rice had ploughed a defiantly independent path to get to where he was, releasing his album O on his own DRM label and organising his own gigs, another pair of routes that Sheeran would take. What's more, the songs on O were largely inspired by Rice's relationship with Dublin-born musician Lisa Hannigan, who also sang on the album. The pair fell in love during the making of the record: 'That had just kind of happened through the making of O,' Rice later explained in a rare interview with Ireland's *Hot Press* music paper. 'So the record felt like a record of creativity and love, and just that whole sense of coming together with a bunch of people – and in particular with Lisa. We just worked really well together. I loved her taste. Whenever I'd do something and she'd comment on it, most of the time I'd just completely agree. We just were very, very compatible: in the studio, on the stage. But when that relationship changed it just made it very difficult because we never had the space from each other, to get used to the change.'

Again, there would be a connection to Ed's work. Sheeran's + album would also be centred on his relationship with one person, his childhood sweetheart Alice. Rice's influence was so great that it was something Ed would rarely fail to mention in virtually every interview he did after he began to gain attention. Sheeran's highlighting of Rice and the way his music informed his own work has done a lot to send Ed's fans in the Irishman's direction.

The 'Cannonball' video would stir Ed into immediate action: 'The next day I went out and bought his album O,' he later explained to journalist Tom Doyle. 'I remember coming home and sitting in my room with my JVC CD player and listening to [second track] 'Volcano' over and over again. I couldn't get past that song. It was the intimacy and the way he conveyed emotions.'

At the age of 11 Ed Sheeran's life had taken a dramatic turn. Music began to dominate, but what happened next would make him feel that music was something that he could not only enjoy, but that he could create himself.

TWO

TYPICAL AVERAGE TEEN

Ed Sheeran had one major asset when it came to pursuing his new-found passion for music: his dad John. He was happy to encourage his son's interest in music by taking him to see bands – often travelling to London to see major events. 'He was a cool dad,' Sheeran told *The Mail* in 2011. 'The first live gig I went to was Green Day at Wembley, though I thought seeing people like Paul McCartney and Bob Dylan was even cooler.'

Music began to take over. Schoolwork began to suffer. Homework in particular was something Ed began to view as being 'petty'. Instead of fighting him over it, John Sheeran took a different approach: 'I never did homework because I was always into music,' Ed would later explain to MSN. 'So he went, Right, instead of doing homework, I'll

15

take you to a gig and you'll watch how this guy does it and that will inspire you. He brought that side of me out – the worker side.'

The way that one guy in particular did it was to provide an invaluable lesson for Ed. He and his father travelled to Dublin to see the man behind his favourite album: Damien Rice. Rice was performing at the city's famous Whelan's venue on Wexford Street. In 2012 Ed would appear at Whelan's himself, joining his cousin Laura Sheeran onstage to accompany her spooky electronica with some human beatboxing.

It was a common occurrence for the Sheerans to be travelling to and from Ireland with their many family connections, so to be able to combine that with a gig was a bonus. 'All my cousins are scattered around Wexford, Dublin, Cork and Galway,' the singer later told Ireland's *Sunday World* newspaper. 'I've always been going back and forth to Ireland to visit family.'

What struck Ed most about the gig was how self-contained Rice was as a performer. Simplicity was everything – less really was more. He'd later describe seeing the Irishman as 'an epiphany'. Ed: 'I loved how he would get up on stage with just an acoustic guitar and display his emotions.'

Rice's musical stock in trade was baring his soul. His image was that of the broken-hearted troubadour: 'I had this sense about me at the time, and so if somebody did me wrong in a relationship then it was like, Grrrr! You know, I'd pick up the guitar and I'd write about it,' he explained to Irish music paper *Hot Press* about his writing methods. 'I look back at a lot of the songs and the person who wrote them, they are nearly all coming from the point of view of victimhood. You know, how could you do that to me?'

Rice's performance that night stopped Sheeran in his tracks, but what happened after the gig was over was more than he could have hoped for. 'Afterwards, we stuck around and Damien and his band came into the pub next door. I didn't have much to say – I was too young.' Perhaps sensing the youngster's shyness, Rice tried to connect with him in a different way. He drew the 11-year-old a picture – it showed Ed with a plane zooming over his head. Years later, Sheeran would make a permanent record of the meeting by having the drawing turned into a tattoo on his arm.

Seeing Rice convinced Ed that one man and a guitar could hold a room: 'It was inspiring seeing him on stage for two hours with just an acoustic guitar and his voice. Being able to command a crowd like that made me think, Wow, it can be done. That night when I got home, I wrote six songs, my first six songs.'

Ed says that his first ever song was based on a chord sequence 'borrowed' from a Green Day song. 'When you're 11 years old you're allowed to plagiarise!' he later told *Total Guitar* magazine. One song from this first batch was called 'Typical Average' – precocious stuff for an 11-year-old. 'It was the typical "I'm a normal teen, do you know what I mean?" stuff,' he would later recall, with a slight squirm. 'I wrote loads of songs when I was young. They weren't very good.'

Even at the age of 11, Ed managed to conjure up a rather world-weary view of life in his song 'Typical Average'. It also saw the start of a technique he would use in the future: putting himself as a character into his songs. However, in the case of his first effort, the listener has to allow for a little poetic licence on Sheeran's part. He sings about his drunken mental state and the fact that his friends don't trust him. This is the kind of stuff that was fine from the likes of Damien Rice – he was a nearly 30 at the time – but a little odd coming from an 11-year-old. 'An 11 or 12-year-old doesn't really write about anything,' Sheeran later admitted to the website *Access Hollywood*. 'They just make words rhyme. That's pretty much what the songs were. They were awful songs but it was good groundwork.'

Nonetheless, Sheeran took the view that regardless of the initial quality of his tunes, the more songs you wrote, the better you became as a songwriter. He came up with a neat analogy for the creative process in an interview with the *Daily Mail*, comparing it to being, 'Like turning on a tap in an old house. First you'll get the mud and dirty water, but the more you get it out, the quicker the good water starts flowing.'

The Dublin experience energised the 11-year-old. The songs began to come a little faster. He'd later admit that his first efforts were directly inspired by other people's songs, telling the *Daily Telegraph*: 'I picked up a few chords and quite quickly started writing my own songs using other people's chord structures.'

Some of those chords were clearly Damien Rice's. Ed

would take every opportunity possible to flag up Rice's influence, even name checking him in the song 'You Need Me, I Don't Need You'. But the Dublin gig was the only time Sheeran would see him live: 'I'd love to see him again,' he later quipped to journalist Andy Welch, 'but he might sue me because I'm very influenced by him.'

In September 2002 Ed started at secondary school at Framlingham's Thomas Hills High, a school named after a prominent local businessman and philanthropist who died in 1703. The school motto is: 'Truth, The Daughter of Time'. The school specialises in technology, languages and the arts and has a particularly good reputation for music, supporting several orchestras and choirs.

By time Ed arrived at the school, the first of the *Harry Potter* films had been released and with his shock of red hair, the new kid was immediately likened to actor Rupert Grint. 'I went to school and obviously was a ginger kid,' Ed later told the Reuters news agency, 'so you're obviously going to get the Ron Weasley comments at some point.'

Despite this, Ed was confident enough in his budding musicianship to offer to play in front of his new schoolmates, his first ever gig: 'I was 11 and it was at my school's charity rock concert,' he later recalled in an interview with the *Daily Mail*. 'I played "Layla" by Eric Clapton on an acoustic guitar. I was new at the school, a short little ginger kid with those blue plastic NHS glasses. I didn't want to go on stage, but I did and it was fun. No one could have said a bad word, because I was so young and enthusiastic.'

There would be one member of staff in particular who didn't have a bad word for Ed. Despite the youngster not being an ideal student, the music department spotted his potential early on: 'I was never really that good at school and could not really concentrate,' Sheeran later told the *Ipswich Star*. 'I started working hard at music because I was not working hard at anything else. I had a music teacher called Richard Hanley. He was an inspirational teacher for me and he is definitely one of the cogs in the machine.'

'He's being very generous and kind there,' Richard Hanley told me. 'I can't claim any responsibility at all. All I did was give him the space and the opportunity to perform and gently and quietly support him when we could. It's very kind of him to remember us.'

Richard Hanley has been at Thomas Mills since 1990 but describes himself as one of the 'younger members of staff'. He's now director of music at the school. One of his responsibilities is laying on school concerts; his pupil Ed Sheeran soon became a regular fixture at these events. As Ed's musical confidence grew, he became bold enough to move on from Eric Clapton's 'Layla' and began to perform his own songs: 'We'd say, Right the Christmas concert is coming up, Ed – would you like to perform something?' Richard Hanley recalls. 'He'd get up and perform one of his songs and everyone would be sitting there amazed. That's how it worked. We gave him the freedom and flexibility to get on with it. I didn't advise him on his compositions at all, we just provided the supportive atmosphere. He was very prolific. There didn't seem to be a prolonged agonised period of composition – that might have happened in the background – he just seemed to be able to do it and produce songs, perform them and get on with it.'

At the age of 12, Ed was also appearing in school stage productions on a regular basis. He played Officer Krupke in *West Side Story* alongside his brother Matthew, who played Detective Schrank. He also appeared in *Grease* and *The Sound of Music*.

Away from school Ed was also in demand as a performer at family weddings – and with his extended Anglo-Irish family, these were in plentiful supply. 'The first time I saw Ed was at his aunt's wedding, who lives in Skibbereen in Ireland,' recalls Ed's cousin Gordon Burns. 'She was getting married and the reception was in her fantastic house on top of a cliff overlooking the ocean. After the speeches these two kids played some music. One kid with a shock of red hair – obviously Ed with his guitar – and the other was his cousin Laura. She did a quite interesting piece, stamping a rhythm on the ground. She's now making her way in the music industry too. As far as Ed was concerned, I can't remember going away thinking, Wow that kid is going to be a star. Kids are always good at weddings, aren't they? Oh isn't that lovely?'

It wasn't the only time that Ed would play the cute card to his advantage. He would also take the opportunity to busk when he was in Ireland to earn some extra money: 'I'd go out on Grafton Street in Dublin,' Ed later told the *Wall Street Journal*. 'You'd just get people giving you money because you were cute.'

Meanwhile, Ed's guitar playing was coming along at a remarkable pace, but he wanted to take it to the next level, really push himself. What he did next would be the first of a series of bold moves on Ed's part, actions designed to get him where he wanted be.

As his musical tastes widened, he'd become fascinated by the playing of New York-born guitarist Preston Reed, who'd developed a two-handed, percussive style of playing that had energised acoustic players around the world. No simple strumming for Preston Reed – by tapping the guitar strings, banging on the guitar body and fretting his instrument with his hand over rather than under the neck, he creates a whole band out of one instrument. Or as Reed's own website puts it: 'Preston Reed is a one-man revolution. The New Yorker tweaks the nose of musical convention, pokes the eye of accepted wisdom, and burns the rulebook of the past. His unique style is impossible, unfathomable, unthinkable, as with blurred hands he taps, tickles, slaps and soothes his instrument, fusing polyrhythmic percussion with emotive melody to create a sonic landscape. Each piece is a symphonic tidal wave, yet Reed only needs one acoustic and ten fingers to send it crashing onto audiences across the planet.'

Total Guitar magazine once said of Reed that he is 'widely thought of as the world's most gifted guitarist' – a quote you'll find proudly displayed on the Preston Reed website. British musicians like Newton Faulkner and Ben Howard have taken Reed's tapping style on board and incorporated into their own music.

Irish singer-songwriter Gary Dunne – who would himself be a major influence on Ed's music – told me how smitten the Sheerans were with Reed's flamboyant performing style. 'When I first met Ed and his dad John they were always banging on about Preston Reed.' Yet Ed's music is known for its stripped-down sound – it's hard to believe that he was looking to be a virtuoso on the guitar. 'It's not my kind of thing at all, I'm not into virtuosity,' agrees Dunne. 'I don't get it. Virtuosity is like footballers doing keepy-uppys.'

Ed contacted Reed and barely into his teens, he flew out to the States to meet him and learn more about his extravagant guitar style. Ed Sheeran was making it clear to those around him that he was taking his musical ambitions very seriously indeed. 'That was just phenomenal really,' recalls Richard Hanley when asked about Ed's trip to see Reed. 'He knew this guitarist and performer so he went to America and spent time being taught and working with him. To have the presence of mind at that age to know that's what you wanted to do and where you want to go – and to take yourself off and do it – was fantastic.'

Ed's visit to the States and his period of 'study' with Reed is not something he has highlighted in the intervening years. It's hard to hear any aspect of Reed's playing in Ed's guitar style today – other than perhaps the idea of being a 'one-man band'. Reed uses his virtuosity to create the idea that there were several people playing at once; Ed would use technology.

As Ed's musical horizons broadened, so did his ambitions.

He tried being part of a band – playing Guns N' Roses cover versions – but working alone seemed to suit him better. He asked a local pub if he could perform there: 'I was about 14 when I played to the bar staff and was told to "turn it down",' he later told *EP1zine*. 'How rock 'n' roll, eh?' Despite this, more gigs followed. Richard Hanley: 'He had every opportunity to perform at school concerts and he took every opportunity to perform gigs locally and more widely too.'

Soon the teenager was playing a gig a month in and around Suffolk, using MySpace to publicise what he was up to. Richard Hanley: 'His use of the internet is crucial – getting his songs out there. My two children are a similar age to Ed and they followed him on the web at first and then started going to his gigs.'

These days, there is an ongoing strain of bickering among Sheeran fans along the lines of 'I was into Ed before you were'. Richard Hanley's daughter Lizi could probably lay claim to being one of Sheeran's longest-serving admirers. 'The first time I saw Ed live was at a school concert,' she told me. 'I'd gone because it was Dad's concert and I saw him do a cover of the Nizlopi song "Love Is". He must have been about 14. It just blew me away. I remember Dad saying that he did gigs around and about Ipswich and Suffolk and that's what made me think, "I'll check him out." I've seen him playing in lots of little venues and clubs, which I feel really lucky to have done now. Because we were the same sort of age I looked at him and thought, God you're young! His lyrics were great – he's young but the lyrics are quite old. I remember Dad saying so many times, "If only he gets his head down he could go really far." Dad said he wasn't the best student to have because he was doing gigs rather than doing coursework. That was what was important to him. But he did work incredibly hard and he deserves the success he's had. It was nice knowing secretly that I know this really cool guy and no one else does. You love it when you discover something musically, when you go to a little gig that no one else knows about. It's great. And I still like him now.'

Ed's mum and dad John and Imogen were also usually at these early gigs to listen to their son and lend their support and encouragement. Sometimes they were the only ones there. 'They were the first ones to encourage me,' Ed later told journalist Anthony Bond. 'They have been really encouraging since day one and they come to as many gigs as they can.'

As the gigs increased school work at Thomas Mills inevitably took a back seat: 'The education is good but it often clashes with the music,' Ed explained to BBC Suffolk while he was still at the school. 'Sometimes I have to take two or three weeks off for recording or for gigs, and often get back really late and go to school the next morning.'

Richard Hanley says the school began to realise that mainstream education wasn't for his star musical pupil: 'We were very accepting. One of the things about Ed was that he was really focussed and committed right from the very beginning. The determination to do it and to get there was really very strong. His parents were very upfront about it, they negotiated time with the school.'

Ed wanted to record some of the songs he was writing, but the facilities at Thomas Mills were too basic for what he wanted to achieve. Richard Hanley: 'His parents were incredibly supportive and he was able to use local recording studios because the facilities we had here were not up to the job.' Ed found facilities in Framlingham and collated his songs into a demo. His confidence in the songs was strong enough to convince him that there could be a wider audience for them – he decided to sell copies of the demo at school. The experience gave him the nerve to send a copy to singer-songwriter Lisa Hannigan, Damien Rice's muse and collaborator on the *O* album. In 2011 Ed revisited the demo to see if time had been kind to it. In his opinion, it hadn't: 'It sounds like a cat being drowned,' he told the *Daily Record*. 'I won't be releasing it any time soon.'

But there were songs from this period that were deemed good enough to appear on a five-track EP known as the *Orange Room*. Although it's always listed in Sheeran's discography, it is a notoriously difficult CD to get hold of. The songs on the EP – including 'Typical Average' – have a folky, Oasis lilt to them, ironic given his previously stated claim that Britpop wasn't an influence on him because he was too young. They were all written between 2002 and 2004 and the CD was 'released' – that is to say Sheeran began selling it – in 2005.

It's fascinating to hear these songs in the context of Ed's career to date. They simultaneously sound just like him... yet nothing like him at all. On the self-reverential track

'Moody Ballad of Ed' in particular Sheeran sounds like a teenage Liam Gallagher, and the track includes a very Noel Gallagher-like guitar solo. 'Misery' is a low-key acoustic piece with a light vocal that breaks out into another mid-paced Oasis sound-alike. 'Addicted' is most recognisable as a Sheeran track and features some rather hopeful falsetto vocals. Final track 'I Love You' is cut from very similar cloth to 'Addicted', with shimmering cymbals and acoustic strums dominating before the Britpop guitars chime in. The singing is hesitant, the lyrics are of the eyes/lies, fast/last, much/touch variety and the playing is straightforward, but for a boy in his early teens it's a strong – if not world-shattering – start.

Ed was still involved in every level of music at his school, including school trips in the UK and abroad. He went to Salzburg in Austria as part of a tour of places of musical interest. Even after a day of music, he was still up for more. 'In the evenings when we'd finished all the concerts and everyone was relaxing, Ed would get the guitar out and have a sing-along,' remembers Richard Hanley.

Staff and teachers at Thomas Mills had by now come to rely on Ed to perform at school events, and the 2006 Christmas show was no exception. Alongside performances of the theme from the *Pink Panther* and 'Somewhere Over the Rainbow', Ed performed one of his own songs.

Looking at those school programmes now, it's possible to track Ed's early musical progress and see how quickly he was progressing. The following year, the entry in the School Christmas Concert programme was an unusual one. Not every child could boast a mention in the school show that would read: 'Ed Sheeran – Song From Latest Album'.

Confidence in his abilities was now beyond question.

THREE

WHAT WAS THAT THING YOU USED?

By this stage Ed had made a decision that music was where his future would lie – or at the very least, he saw himself involved in the world of 'entertainment'.

By his mid-teens he seems to have adopted something of a scattergun approach, trying a variety of means to achieve his ends. At 15 he joined the National Youth Music Theatre, with an eye on becoming an actor rather than a musician. Based in London, the NYMT is a stage workshop that mounts musical productions for teenage wannabe performers. Ex pupils include *Little Britain's* Matt Lucas, *Billy Elliot* star Jamie Bell and actor Jude Law, who is the theatre's patron. It's perhaps best described as a more actorly, traditional version of the BRIT School, which has produced the likes of Adele, Amy Winehouse and Rizzle Kicks.

Joining the NYMT connected Sheeran to a loop of opportunities designed to appeal to young performing hopefuls. Ed started to get regular emails about forthcoming auditions. One of these asked for young people who could 'sing, play the guitar and act' to try out for a new television show being prepared by Granada Television called *Britannia High*. 'The show itself was meant to be a mix between *Skins* and *High School Musical*,' Ed later explained to Absolute Radio. The description of the show – and the kind of performers they were looking for – seemed to suit Ed down to the ground. 'I wanted to be an actor – I played guitar and I sung but I wanted to be an actor.'

The producers were looking for 'triple threat' performers who could sing, dance and act; they wanted performers who could be 'stars on the television, stars in the pop charts and stars in arenas'.

Getting involved with the show as an actor nearly ended Sheeran's music career before it really started. It's easy to see how the series would have appealed to him – on paper it looked like the show couldn't lose. It had the songs, some penned by Take That's Gary Barlow and Robbie Williams's collaborator Guy Chambers; it had the choreography, by Arlene Phillips of Hot Gossip and *Strictly Come Dancing* fame; and it had cutting-edge interactive elements that were a real novelty at the time – podcasts, social media content and online tutorials so fans could learn to dance and act like the stars of the show. It couldn't lose.

One of the show's characters was called Jez Tyler; he's the sensitive singer-songwriter type who tells his dad he's enrolled in a business school when in fact he's signed on at *Britannia High*. It seemed tailor-made for the likes of Ed Sheeran. 'I got into the final four,' he later explained to Digital Spy. 'Pixie Lott was in it (she auditioned but also didn't get a part). I said, "If I get this, I'll stop the singing and properly do the acting thing."' By the same token, he also vowed that if he didn't get the part, he'd take it almost as a 'sign' that he should stick to singing. 'I had a lot of fun doing the auditions. I learnt a lot.'

Sadly one thing Ed didn't learn was how to dance. A documentary was made about the making of the series, following the fortunes of the final 40 hopefuls looking to grab the six main parts on offer. Pixie Lott can be seen looking bright and perky in the front row getting a pep talk about what's expected of them, while Sheeran is relegated to the back – the programme producers evidently seeing him as an also-ran.

A slim and short-haired Ed is also seen in the audition stages singing Nizlopi's 'All My Life' and being praised for his vocal skills. He's also seen clod-hopping about like a baby elephant as he attempts to move in time to Justin Timberlake's 'Like I Love You'. Ed stamps his feet, waves his arms about and looks like he's wandered into the wrong room. 'Not even an option,' was Arlene Phillips's view of Ed's dancing abilities. 'Eventually we're going to have to find some people who can dance.' Although it's fashionable to claim that *Britannia High* was a dreadful flop, viewing figures for the series actually held steady at around the six million mark when it was finally broadcast in October

2008, and it was sold to countries around the world. A second series wasn't commissioned when it finished nine weeks later – in May the following year *Glee* first aired and became a worldwide phenomenon. 'I wasn't really serious [about] doing music at the time, and then when I didn't get in I was just kinda like Screw it, I'll start singing properly,' Ed later told *The Scotsman*.

Ed's more exhibitionist side still had an outlet though, despite not getting the *Britannia High* job. Around this time he filmed a series of videos of himself showing off some of his other skills and posted them on YouTube. He performed the theme music from the James Bond movies by tapping out the notes on a series of half-filled wine glasses and a jug of juice, and he indulged his sweet tooth in by seeing how many sweets and cakes he could stuff into his mouth. In the aptly titled 'How Many Can You Fit in Your Mouth Challenge?' videos, viewers saw Ed – assisted by his friend Stephen – shoving as many Maltesers, marshmallows, gummy mix and Mr Kipling lemon slices into his mouth as he could before either laughter or his gag reflex prevented him from continuing. It's all pretty harmless stuff. For the record, Ed's tally was 41 Maltesers, 23 marshmallows, 37 gummies and six lemon slices.

If he wasn't going to be an actor – or a professional sweet and cake eater – then it was back to concentrating on music. While Ed's flirtation with acting was going on, a musical interest was growing, one that would rival even his love of Damien Rice. As with Rice, Ed never failed to flag up his debt to this act in later life, but to many this influence was a more surprising one. But on closer inspection, the similarities between Sheeran's work and that of the acoustic duo he latched onto are even more pronounced. In some circles, it's hard to think of a less fashionable name to drop than that of Nizlopi. That didn't deter Sheeran at the time and still doesn't deter him: 'For me they were the best band of that time,' he told Absolute Radio, 'and they were independent.'

Nizlopi – singer and guitarist Luke Concannon and double-bass player John Parker from Leamington Spa – were probably the least likely 'underground folk hip hop band' ever to have a Number 1 hit single. When Sheeran came across them they'd just self-released their debut album called *Half These Songs Are About You*, a title sure to appeal to the young singer-songwriter. The album contained a track called 'JCB' – better known as the 'JCB Song' – which was released in the summer of 2005 and scraped into the UK Top 200. Later that year it went to Number 1 after being championed by Radio 2's Dermot O'Leary and by the viral buzz created by its accompanying cartoon video. The song was not really about heavy machinery at all: 'The single is based on a true story,' Concannon later explained to the *Daily Mail*. 'My family run a construction firm, building roads. As a youngster, I'd often sit in the [JCB] diggers with my dad. We'd have a great laugh, singing songs and holding up the traffic as we drove down country roads. It's a song about memories, essentially. It's about me feeling proud of my dad, but also about the emotions of a five-year-old boy who is having a tough time with bullies at school. Sitting in my dad's digger was a release from that.'

Ed Sheeran is clear where the band and its lead singer stands in his affections: 'Luke Concannon is my childhood hero. I owe a large amount of my career to him.'

The novelty nature of the 'JCB Song' would overshadow the achievements of Nizlopi elsewhere – they were extraordinarily proficient musicians, using a combination of acoustic guitar, stand-up bass, human beatbox and sheer charm to win over audiences with their rum mix of folk, blues, jazz and beats. Concannon in particular is a singularly uninhibited performer, musically creative and charmingly eccentric in the way he approaches what he does: 'We celebrate people doing what they love,' he says by way of an explanation of what Nizlopi are all about. 'Not giving in to our bullshit culture that is deathly, but creating what we believe in, and feck the experts and authorities. We celebrate love and the community, rockin' it. And doing rudies. And joy.'

There are many aspects of Concannon as a performer that can be seen in Ed Sheeran's stage persona. First, there's his singing: Concannon's voice has a yearning, pleading tone that can be clearly heard in Sheeran's vocals. Then there's Concannon's brand of stage presence: the Nizlopi singer demands audience interaction and participation. He will happily drag audience members on stage to help out with songs, leap into the audience to perform without amplification or even perform at fans' houses before or after gigs. Ed Sheeran was smitten by Concannon and the music of Nizlopi and began working out how to play their songs note for note: 'I was a bigger fan of them than I was of Damien Rice,' Ed later confessed to *Q* magazine. 'Like, completely obsessed. They had two albums and four EPs and I could sit down and sing and play you every single song without fail.'

Ed began to follow the duo around the country, tipping up wherever they played and soaking up their summery, feel-good music. In Nizlopi's most famous song Concannon sings about his joy about not being in school, spending his time doing what he wants to do. Sheeran began to take a similar view and began to skip school to see the duo. With the summer holidays coming up, Ed spotted that Nizlopi were about to go on tour. He began a sustained email campaign, asking if he could help out in whatever capacity he could. To his surprise, Nizlopi's tour manager said yes. Ed's ever-supportive parents gave him the go-ahead and at the age of just 15, Ed Sheeran became Nizlopi's guitar technician. 'It was sick,' he told *Q* magazine, 'but also in the process, without realising it, I learned how to perform live and sing and project my voice and write songs, just by being around them.'

As he travelled from gig to gig in the band's van, Sheeran watched and learned. He became, in his view, a good roadie. He learned about guitars, venues and the wisdom of never drinking before you went on stage. He also learned how to be a professional, working musician: 'That experience – seeing how they performed, how they interacted with their fans and how professional they were backstage – was the foundation for what's happening to me now,' he later explained to the *Daily Mail*. 'It's all about hard work, graft and being nice to people. That's the best way to do it.'

The lessons that Ed soaked up that summer would stand him in good stead in the years to come. The positivity of Nizlopi and their relationship with their fans would have a profound effect on the 15-year-old. Ed took the following lesson with him from the experience: 'Always be in a good mood, even if you're in a bad mood. If you see fans after the show, even if you've had a bad show, you have to be cool, rather than negative.'

Nizlopi would put Ed in such a good mood that he wrote a song about them: 'Two Blokes and a Double Bass', which is 94-second-long love letter to the duo which would later appear on Ed's *Want Some* album. The song also namechecks one act that Sheeran saw while following Nizlopi around the country: Irish singer-songwriter Gary Dunne. Dunne supported Nizlopi at their Shepherd's Bush Empire gig in London; Ed and his dad went to the gig and the teenager was immediately taken with the historic venue. He told his dad that one day he'd like to play here – John Sheeran clearly believed very strongly in his son's burgeoning talent and told him that not only would he play the venue one day, he'd sell it out. Seven years later, he did.

Gary Dunne had recently released his debut album *Twenty Twenty Fiction* and was carving a name for himself as a robust live performer. Dunne had recently started experimenting with a 'looping' effects pedal, whereby a musician can record their guitar and their voice and immediately play it back live to a make a musical and rhythmic loop of sound. 'It records everything live and plays it back so there's no need for backing tracks,' Ed later explained to viewers of the BBC's *Blue Peter* programme, when he appeared on the show to explain the technique. 'It's all live and off the cuff.'

Scottish singer KT Tunstall had become a star overnight after using a loop pedal on Jools Holland's *Later* programme in 2004, a performance that Ed saw on TV. In the right hands, looping was a devastating live technique. Once again, Sheeran was bowled over and immediately saw the potential benefits that looping could bring to his stage performances.

Gary Dunne explained to me how he came to use the looping pedal, and how he inadvertently set Ed off in a new musical direction that would become a key part of his sound: 'In 2001 I was touring with New York songwriter Joseph Arthur – I got half of the opening slots, Damien Rice got the other half. Arthur got up with an acoustic guitar and this crazy live looping set up and just blew me away. In his live show he creates these massive, epic psychedelic live loops... then puts down his guitar and paints a picture live on stage! He takes it to the next level. I just couldn't believe it. It's a completely different style of performing. It was like having a black pen and a red pen – and then suddenly having all the colours. I can be up there on my own on stage and I can draw everything.

'I went straight out, researched the whole thing, picked

up a thing called a Boss Loop Station – the same one that Ed uses – got into it and hibernated for six months to a year with an acoustic guitar plugged into a practice amp and just built grooves and songs and then went back out onto the London circuit. I didn't know anyone else who was doing it in London at the time – it was like working with a whole new tool box and I wrote a whole new set of songs. It was a whole new way of working. I was on tour with Nizlopi – who you probably know from the "JCB Song". Incredible guys, serious songwriters – I was doing Shepherd's Bush Empire and that was when I was really on fire with the looping. Ed saw me when I was really excited and passionate about looping. Ed was there with his dad. He was 15 at the time and he really got into my stuff.'

Soon after the gig, Dunne was contacted by the Sheerans with an invite to come to Framlingham and play his music at their house: 'John Sheeran emailed a few weeks later and said, "My son's a songwriter, he saw you play, what was that thing you used?" And then he asked would I come and play at Ed's 16th birthday party.'

Sheeran has been nothing if not upfront about why he wanted Dunne to come and play at his house: 'I MySpaced him after the gig purely for the fact that I wanted to see how it all worked up close and personal,' he told the music website OurVinyl TV in 2012. 'He did a gig for my friends and they all bought CDs – that's how he got paid. He stayed, we chatted, he taught me the loop pedal.'

Dunne was picked up from Ipswich train station by Ed and John Sheeran and driven to their home in

Framlingham. 'They are good people,' says Dunne about meeting the Sheerans. 'They're solid music fans, really passionate about music.'

'House gigs', like the one Dunne was preparing to play at Ed's home, are a common way for acoustic performers to earn a living in between tours and are normally fairly low-key affairs. Dunne was amazed at what he saw when he arrived at the Sheerans: 'Even at that age Ed was probably more driven than I was,' Dunne says. 'He had gathered 40 or 50 of his teenage friends packed into their house and Ed had brought in a PA and lighting – he was just on the ball. Normally you rock up at someone's house and it can be completely shit or it can be amazing, and Ed had really pulled out all the stops. He just wanted to run a proper gig at his house. The kids seemed to really like it. We stayed up really late and Ed videoed the gig, deconstructed all the songs and got me to teach him all the parts and how to use the loop station.'

Seeing Dunne use his loop pedal up close would have a profound effect on Ed. 'I bought one the next day and I've been using it ever since,' he later explained in an interview with *Nerve* magazine, For those of a technical nature, the loop that Sheeran used is a Boss RC-20 – later a RC-30 – and Ed has probably done more to popularise looping than anyone else. 'It doesn't take that long to learn,' Ed later told BBC Nottingham when asked about the technique. 'But it took about four years to get the timing right and get a sixth sense about when to press it without looking down. That took a while to do, but it came ... with lots of gigs.'

Lizi Hanley – who first saw Sheeran perform at a school concert – also saw some of those early 'looping' gigs: 'The way he played guitar – I'd never seen anyone play guitar like that before,' she told me. 'He was playing with a loop pedal, which I'd never seen before. That shows how talented he was – the fact that he could play all these layers and do it live.'

Ironically, it wouldn't be too long before Gary Dunne got rid of his loop pedal – in fact, he sold it to Ed. 'I was becoming known as "the guy who did the looping" and that didn't sit comfortably with me. I'm a songwriter and the colours and potential that looping gives you obviously can restrict you too. I stopped looping as my primary thing about five years ago. I didn't want to be The Looping Guy... plus everyone started doing it. And 90 per cent of it was shite.'

Sheeran was such a Dunne fan that he put together the videos he took of the performer at his 16th birthday party and posted them online. It was another indicator of things to come: 'He ended up running my MySpace for a while,' Dunne told me. 'He was always into social media and had it nailed from day one.'

By his mid-teens Sheeran had worked out a mixture of style and content that suited him down the ground, pulling in a diverse range of influences from his musical interests: the open-hearted, communal vibe of Damien Rice, the beats, improvisation and people skills of Nizlopi, the 'one man band' stylings of Preston Reed and the hypnotic loops of Gary Dunne.

It's fair to say that it was a template no one else would be likely to copy. It's also reasonable to point out that Sheeran doesn't forget where his influences have come from. In September 2011 he played the Shepherd's Bush Empire, this time as the headliner: his handpicked support acts were Gary Dunne and Luke Concannon.

Gary Dunne: 'I'm very comfortable with being a strong influence on Ed. He's been very open about how he was inspired by what I do and how it opened up creative doors for him. He acknowledges it and that's an honour. When creative people are starting out – I'm not calling myself Ed's hero here – but you aspire to be like your heroes and you copy people and then you find your voice. If my looping is a major influence then there are licks and phrases in Ed's songs that are just … Luke. That pleading, longing thing. It's great. But Ed's still very young and he's got that grimey, R&B thing going on that's nothing to do with me and Luke. Ed was very clearly and openly inspired by what I did and even now that he's huge he's still open about it. It still sells albums for me. I suppose I'd be a bit pissed off if he'd become huge and he'd been so clearly influenced by the way I create music and he was in denial about it. Then it would be a bit different. But he's a great guy and he's wonderfully supportive of what I do. I'm absolutely fine with that.'

Perhaps inspired by the Nizlopi and Dunne experience, Ed put together another collection of songs on a second self-funded release, the *Ed Sheeran Album*. The songs are altogether slicker in terms of the playing, singing and production than the *Orange Room* EP. On 'Open Your

Ears' Ed's previously faltering falsetto is now bang on target. The Oasis guitars have gone. In their place there are discreet strings and on an emotional level it's an altogether more Damien Rice affair. On songs like 'Insomniac's Lullaby' – a song perhaps inspired by those late nights staying up surfing the TV channels – the lyrical content has stepped up too. The rhyming dictionary seems to have been put aside but Sheeran sings about being kept awake because he's not 'your man', a presumptuous lyric for a lad so young (the track was written in 2005). 'Quiet Ballad of Ed' sees Sheeran self-referencing again in a Rice-style confessional song. There's involvement from Ed's family too with cousin Laura Sheeran on vocals and Jethro Sheeran – otherwise known as Alonestar – collaborating on 'Pause', the first time we see a glimpse of the Ed to come. The dreamy balladeering is left behind in favour of an acoustic hip hop vibe with a swift rap from his cousin. This new groove doesn't last long and it's back to downbeat strumming for 'The Sea'. Then there's a genuine surprise towards the end – we are suddenly in the middle of a Simon and Garfunkel pastiche: 'Way Home' has the lyrical thrust of 'Homeward Bound' attached to the tune of 'Scarborough Fair'. It's a clever exercise in mimicking the sounds of his parents' record collection more than anything else. Bringing up the rear is an aptly titled bonus track called 'Bonus Track', a low key summery piece of jazz that doesn't stay around long enough to concern us that Sheeran's music is taking a more lounge-y direction.

Ed continued gigging and used his live shows as an

opportunity to sell copies of his new CD to the scattering of people who attended. He also managed to convince some local shops to take them, even selling some as far afield as the seaside town of Aldeburgh. It was another small step in the right direction. Every opportunity had to be seized. Around this time, Ed made a slight return to the stage and got involved with the Suffolk Youth Theatre. The theatre group runs summer schools for budding performers as well as staging larger, more 'classical' or well known shows once a year as their main house production.

Ed auditioned for a part in a production of the 17th-century Spanish play *Fuente Ovejuna*. It tells the stirring tale of the villagers of Fuente Ovejuna, who kill an evil army commander and take collective responsibility for the act. Fellow cast member Joe Doran told me about the youth theatre and Ed's part in the production: 'It's an amateur drama group for 12 to 18-year-olds and every year they'd put on a performance at the Wolsey Theatre in Ipswich. There was always a large cast, lots of young people and they were ensemble shows, lots of singing and we'd always have musicians playing on stage. That's where I met Ed. He had a speaking part but he was also going to play guitar. The play was set in Spain and it had a lot of acoustic music in it.'

Ed began attending rehearsals for the play but his famous work ethic clearly hadn't quite kicked in at this stage. 'It's kind of funny,' says Joe Doran, 'but he didn't seem that focussed on the task of actually learning the music. Believe it or not, he didn't really strike me as a very good musician because he didn't seem to be making much of an effort. At the time he didn't know all the songs he was supposed to be playing. He got told off – properly shouted at – because he didn't seem as dedicated to it as he should have been. I think maybe he was interested in the social side – having a good time with the other performers – so when it came down to actually doing the hard work he earned the ire of our director a couple of times.'

In fact Ed quit the show before the first performance. Joe Doran: 'He dropped out. He never ended up doing the final performance. He said it was the pressure of doing his GCSE – that's what he said when he decided to call it quits.'

Doran still kept tabs on Ed and went to see him live whenever he could: 'First time I saw Ed perform was when he supported Nizlopi at the Norwich Arts Centre. Tiny gig, a few hundred people. It was definitely good. Even at that stage he had a rapport with the audience. He'd tell them he had CDs and merchandise for sale at the back, but he'd do it in a jokey way so you'd laugh rather than resenting him for trying to flog you his wares. He was good, but he definitely got better. I thought at the time, "He deserves to make it."'

With the combination of recording and releasing CDs, playing live, auditioning for TV shows and his borderline stalking of Nizlopi, it's a wonder that Sheeran had time for anything else. But it seems that he did. The pleading, lovelorn nature of the songs on the *Ed Sheeran Album* had an apparent inspiration. Many if not all the songs were for his teenage girlfriend Alice, a Framlingham girl but not, it seems, a fellow pupil at Thomas Mills School. Time and again over the next few years, when asked what a song was about, Ed would reply that it was about his ex girlfriend. 'I had a long-time girlfriend for four years through school,' he later told *Teen Vogue*.

Although he kept the relationship very low key, this aspect of Sheeran's personality would become a key part of his persona when he became a mainstream artist. Ed Sheeran: the singer with the boy-next-door, nice guy image. 'I'm honestly more of a relationship kind of guy,' he later said, squirming slightly at being asked about his love life. 'I'd like to say I'm a rock star, but I'm not. I'm a guy you could take home to meet your mum rather than a guy your mum wouldn't like.'

Though the relationship would last throughout his rise to fame, it wouldn't go beyond his breakthrough success. It would be strained and eventually broken by what happened next in Sheeran's life. The spectre of the romance would always be there though – it would seep into every track on his debut album: 'She's pretty much what the album is all about,' he later told *Q* magazine.

By now, Ed Sheeran knew he wanted to be a musician – he gigged, he recorded, he sold CDs; he *was* a musician. But he wanted more: 'By the time I was 14 or so I thought music was something I'd like to do, and then by 16 I started to think it was something I *could* do,' he later told the *Daily Telegraph*. 'That's when I took all the big risks.'

FOUR

A SECOND FAMILY

Ed was deeply embroiled in preparations for his A levels at school. He was part of a small but competitive, high-achieving group. Tom Rose – now an emerging classical composer – was one of the five youngsters in the Thomas Mills A level group that year. It was tough and many of the drier, theory-based aspects of the course didn't appeal to Ed one bit. 'You are essentially dragging them through the formal bits as best you can,' explains Ed's music teacher Richard Hanley. 'He had to do harmony exercises and dreadful rules of cadence and chord progression and all that sort of thing – that wasn't his thing. His free composition was the area where he shone.'

It was time for Ed to make another bold move to get him to the next stage. At the age of 16, he took the decision to quit school, leave his adopted home town of Framlingham and move to London. It was clear that school was becoming a grind for him – music was the way he expressed himself and that's where his future lay. 'I wasn't really good at anything else if I'm honest!' he told *Nerve* magazine later. 'I really enjoy it – it's a great way to get stuff out of your system. Because you put so much effort into your songs, you really throw your emotions out there – I never get into fights or get angry, I just get really chilled and I think that's why.'

He decided to take the plunge as he was beginning the preparations for his A level course. Richard Hanley told me how the joint pressures of school and Ed's burgeoning career in music had begun to build up: 'Increasingly when he was in the sixth form he was working incredibly hard gigging and taking as many opportunities as he could to perform. He was missing a lot of school for very valid reasons. He works incredibly hard, he's always on the move and he's always performing. That very much started when he was in the sixth form here.'

Ed later explained his reasoning to Radio 1 DJ Zane Lowe: 'With every single profession you need to learn your craft. If you're a doctor you need a degree and you need to learn how to cut people up. If you're a journalist you need to start making tea and working your way up from there. If you're a musician, the only thing you need to learn is how to work a crowd and how to write a song. For me I just needed to do as many gigs as possible. For me, going to university stunts that growth. If I dropped out at 16 and started doing gigs, by the time I was 21 I'd be in a position that most people wouldn't be if they'd gone to uni.'

Ed sat down with his mum and dad and asked them two questions that would have shocked any parents of a 16-year-old: Can I quit school? Can I leave home and move to London? Ed: 'One of my dad's mottos is, nothing ventured, nothing gained. He said that to me from a very, very young age. He basically said, even if you do something and it fails, at least you've had the experience of it, so you might as well just grab life by the balls and just do it.'

He'd later reference his feelings at the time on the song 'You Need Me, I Don't Need You', stating that sadly, Suffolk seemed to suffocate him. Given how young large sections of his subsequent fan base would be, Sheeran has since been at pains to point out that taking his lead and packing in school is not something he would endorse for everyone: 'I think I got all I could out of education. I'm not saying it's the best thing to do for anyone to drop out and pursue music. It was a real gamble; but it did work out and I don't regret it at all.'

At Thomas Mills School, teachers and pupils were shocked, but not actually too surprised at the news of Ed's departure. 'We were sad to see him go,' says Richard Hanley. 'I think it was the best decision in terms of where he wanted to go. I think the schoolwork was getting in the way and holding him back. He wasn't just doing music he was doing other A levels as well and I suppose he was unable to devote time to both his music and his studies – I think that crystallised the decision really. He wanted to get on and now was the time. It was time to move on and take the step. His parents were very supportive and were fantastic throughout.'

But what did John and Imogen Sheeran really think of his decision at the time? 'My mum was different to my dad,' Ed recalled in an interview with his cousin Gordon Burns for BBC Radio Manchester. 'My dad did a similar thing – he basically didn't use his degree at all. He had a degree but he went straight into a job and worked his way up from the bottom to the top. He saw that approach could be applied to the music world. My mum ... well, she's a mum, she wants the best for her son and maybe living on couches for three years isn't the best. For those three years I think she was quite worried.'

Richard Hanley: 'It must have been a hard decision to let him go. It's worked. It produced the results. He's always been very complimentary about the support the school gave him and the flexibility we are able to give him time to fulfil his dream.'

Ed headed off for London – staying initially with a cousin in Bethnal Green – with his effects pedal and a Martin Backpacker guitar, an instrument with an unusual 'baseball bat' shape that's usually used by musicians who want to take their guitar on holiday. But Ed wasn't going away to take it easy and have a good time – he was heading to the capital to work. His mother Imogen was unsurprisingly concerned; no matter how self-contained and confident her son was, he was still only 16. 'I used to worry about him when he first went to London,' she later revealed to the

East Anglian Daily Times. 'But he gained a second family through music who look after him and let me know he's all right. We go to see him play gigs whenever we can.'

Ever the self-starter, Sheeran created this 'second family' himself with his formidable networking skills: 'I knew about three singer-songwriters – they got me started on the scene,' he later explained to the OTUmusic video channel. 'There was a website that listed every single promoter that did acoustic nights and I emailed every single one. There were probably about three hundred of them and I got about 50 replies. I did all those gigs. Then I went back and did them again. And again. And again. And again.'

He would eventually become such a familiar face to the landlords and bar staff on the London open mic circuit that they assumed the confident, assured young musician was at least 18 and would often 'pay' the 16-year-old in booze. Some of these 'payments' would leave a lasting mark on Ed: 'I cannot touch tequila,' he told the Popdust website, recalling one such liquid payday. 'I threw up in a black taxi cab – it did not go down well.' He got paid this way so often he even invented his own foolproof hangover cure: 'Get Coke, shake it up until it gets flat, and down it.'

After creating a buzz back home in Suffolk, he essentially had to start from scratch again in the capital – a massive task for a 16-year-old living away from home for the first time. He later told *Music Week*: 'I had built up a fan base in Ipswich and Norwich but London was an eye opener – you move to London and the grass is not only greener but a massive field and harder to crack.'

At one of his first London gigs, Sheeran had a nightmare experience – but one that he turned around and used to his advantage. During the gig the batteries ran out in his looping effects pedal. The pedal was connected to a microphone to create the vocal samples that drove many of his songs and that shut down too. Age 16, Ed Sheeran was stood on stage in London at one of his earliest shows ... in silence. He had nowhere to go and nowhere to hide. Instinct kicked in: 'I was like, Fuck, what do I do now?' he later recalled. 'I instantly just unplugged and jumped off into the crowd and they all got quiet, so I played the rest of the set acoustic.'

The technique of singing in the middle of an audience was popular among modern-day folk artists to show that they could perform without amplification like their forefathers –that they were authentic, the real deal. It's one thing for a seasoned old folkie to do it, but for a kid of 16 to try it was a bold move. It worked. The crowd fell silent and listened intently to the teenager. It was so successful he began to incorporate it into his set. It was an important moment: 'I realised that you can have that kind of control over people if you just put your foot down I guess. It's your show. At the time I wasn't doing the shows for any other reason other than experience, so even if I was playing to five people, or if the gigs were difficult, it was never a bad thing. Every experience kind of added to the next show and I got to a point where my live performance was polished up, I knew how to connect with different crowds. So it was never really disheartening because I was doing all the gigs to get the experience so when I'm doing bigger gigs, I can just go in and do a great show, hopefully.'

The type of shows he was playing soon began to stretch out beyond the comfort zone of the acoustic circuit and into more alien territory. 'The trick was playing to different audiences, so I wasn't just playing to acoustic crowds,' he told BBC Radio Manchester. 'I was playing to hip hop crowds and comedy crowds and drum and bass crowds, dance crowds and reggae crowds. I've played in front of every crowd imaginable ... and flopped in front of every crowd imaginable. I've learned and you can put me on any stage now and I'll be alright.'

One of his initial contacts when he arrived in London was Chantelle Fiddy, an über-connected blogger and promoter with impeccable contacts in London's grime scene. With its mix of complex time signatures, beats and synthesised basslines, grime had been breaking through since the early noughties via artists like Dizzee Rascal and Wiley. Though he'd shown an interest in the genre since he was at school, Fiddy's music collection was a revelation for folkie Ed: Devlin's *Tales From the Crypt*, Wretch 32's *Teacher Training Day*, Sway DaSafo's *This Is My Demo*. Another music avenue had opened up for him and he consumed it voraciously. The first grime CD he bought was *Playtime Is Over* by Wiley, the east London producer and rapper who was about to taste mainstream success with his 2008 hit 'Wearing My Rolex'. Ed: 'I think it's just the way that they put words together,' he explained to the website I Like Music. 'I mean, singers and songwriters tend to have the same kind of rhyming complex and ways of putting words together and I think the grime flow is really different. They can do it in so many different emotions and flows and ways of bending words, I mean, it's just amazing. As a lyricist, it's something I was just attracted to.'

Ed saw an openness in the grime scene that wasn't so obvious elsewhere – they seemed to 'get him' more than the folkies did. 'I'm just really lucky that I got accepted into that urban grime scene in London when I first moved there, so that has been a big influence on me,' he later told the *Boston Phoenix*. 'I try to make good music without thinking too much about what genre it fits into, which is probably why it comes across quite seamless.' To Sheeran, part of his appeal to the grime scene was the sheer nerve of him showing a face there in the first place: 'The bravery of what I was doing with those shows impressed them, I think – a white, ginger kid from Suffolk going to these nights and having the balls to get up and play.'

At the same time, Sheeran's musical education was also being topped up by more formal means. Surprisingly, he went back to 'school'. He signed up for the London branch of the Access To Music course, enrolling in the Artist Development module at the college's east London site on Stratford High Street. The course is usually only open to musicians over the age of 19. The curriculum is almost a list of things that Sheeran would later excel at: creative planning, target selling, audience analysis, marketing and branding. Sheeran has since become Access To Music's poster boy in terms of successful ex-students – their poster girl is Vanessa White of girl band The Saturdays. 'I loved the freedom,' Ed now says. 'Obviously you are there to learn, but they understood that half of the learning you needed for the industry was outside the classroom with gigs and studio time. It gave me the first push, the opportunity to move to London and the freedom to gig and record whenever I could.'

It was via Access To Music that Sheeran got his first management deal: 'I did a gig at the Norwich Arts Centre,' he explained to BBC Suffolk in 2008, 'and someone at Access To Music put me in contact with Crown Music Management. They've organised a week of recording and when I'm in London they'll organise gigs there as well.'

Crown Music Management has represented the likes of Sugababes, Darius Campbell – better known as infamous *Pop Idol* contestant Darius Danesh – Just Jack, Ellie Goulding and Jessie J. Sheeran was impressed: 'I was at a really young age and I was looking at them as a really big company, thinking you probably know what you're doing,' he later told the BBC. 'So from a young age I was [thinking] I'll try this, I'll try that.'

One thing that was tried was sending Ed off to Surrey to hook up with writer and producer Jake Gosling at his Sticky Studios in Windlesham. It would be the first of several attempts to hone his talent by getting him to collaborate with other writers and musicians. 'This little ginger kid turned up and he was really confident for his age,' Gosling later recalled in an interview with *Sound on Sound* magazine. 'He'd just moved to London and he was living above a pub. We sat down, and we were talking about him moving to London and that became "The City", which was the first thing we wrote together. I felt his lyrics were just insanely good.'

Within the lyrics of 'The City', there are repeated references to Sheeran 'blazing' – smoking weed. Gosling noted that Ed's management at the time weren't too happy about this: 'He thought he couldn't sing about smoking weed, afraid that radio wouldn't play it,' Gosling would later claim in an interview with *The Guardian*. 'But I told him not to worry about that, just to write about what was going on in his life.'

Gosling later blogged in detail about those first recordings and the creative process he and Sheeran generated. 'On each track we tried to find stories and wrote about what was going on with Ed's life and get it all down as quick as we could. The main thing I liked about Ed was that he had so many ideas about his music and what he wanted to do. He also had a real love of urban underground music and could name everyone in the grime scene and had so much respect for these artists. And from his appearance you never would have thought he would!'

With his creative juices flowing, in a real recording studio with a respected producer, Ed could have been forgiven for thinking he had it made and that the big record deal he'd dreamed of was a foregone conclusion: it wasn't. 'My mistake when trying to get into the industry was thinking I'll get signed and make an album at 16 and it just doesn't happen – you really have to work hard,' he told the website

Boundlessology. 'Start at the bottom and work your way up to the top. Just gig as much as you can, write as many songs as you can, and go to live gigs so you can network more. It's not luck when you meet someone; you're in that position because you've put yourself in that position to work your way up.'

Jake Gosling had some words of advice for the 16-year-old: 'He was still young but needed to be directed and told that what he was doing was right and to stick to it and not just sell out.'

While he was working his way up, Ed had produced a new self-made album. He would take copies of *Want Some* to his gigs in a rucksack and sell them to anyone who happened to turn up. 'I'd sell 10 to 20 CDs a night for a tenner. For a kid with a rucksack I did alright.'

There's no grime to be found on *Want Some*. First track 'You Break Me' has the now familiar polite self-revelation and touches of falsetto that had appeared on previous recordings. 'I'm Glad I'm Not You' bears the Nizlopi influence with Sheeran's phrasing aping that of Luke Concannon – the beats are tapped out and looped rather than using drums, in a style reminiscent of Nizlopi. Later in the album Nizlopi would be directly lauded in the song 'Two Blokes and a Double Bass', where Ed sings the duo's praises and namechecks his looping mentor Gary Dunne. In fact a double bass appears on the next track 'You Need to Cut Your Hair', as does a scatting sing/talk style that's reminiscent of Just Jack, otherwise known as musician Jack Allsopp. London-born Allsopp was just breaking through at that time with his album *Overtones* and the accompanying hit single 'Starz in Their Eyes'. Sheeran and Allsopp's fortunes would become entwined over the coming months and years after Sheeran was offered support slots with the musician.

Back on the album, 'Sara' is Sheeran in lovelorn mode as he moons over a girl with blonde hair and blue eyes that all the boys are after. 'Move On' sees the return of his cousin Jethro and a sweary rap about not letting the music industry grind you down – almost an early outing for the themes that would appear later on the song 'You Need Me, I Don't Need You'. 'Yellow Pages', 'Smile' and 'Postcards' are all low-key, downbeat affairs while 'The West Coast of Clare' is the first cover version to appear on one of Sheeran's offerings. The song was originally performed by Irish folk group Planxty and it appears on their self-titled debut released in 1973 – it's easy to imagine the album nestling in Ed's parents' record collection: 'I grew up on Planxty,' he later told Ireland's *Sunday World* newspaper.

The following track 'I Can't Spell' is another first as Sheeran sings without accompaniment. Hidden track 'You Break Me 2' reprises the album's opening track as a piano ballad and works far better than the first version. Apart from this final moment of experimentation, *Want Some* is a remarkably similar collection to the *Ed Sheeran Album*.

Recording by day, playing gigs and selling CDs by night: Sheeran was doing exactly what he'd set out to do in London, though his living conditions were far from ideal. He initially lived in 'a place above a pub with a kebab shop' but was travelling and gigging so often it soon became pointless to have a specific 'home' so he embarked on what would turn out to be an extended period of sofa-surfing – crashing at the homes of friends, contacts or promoters before moving on to the next place. More sensitive souls might think of it as being homeless. Although he claims to have thrived on it there were times when even Sheeran's seemingly indefatigable nature was tested to its limits. There were 'really, really low points where you realise that you have nowhere to stay that night and it's, like, four o'clock in the morning and your phone is dead,' he told OTUmusic. 'That's not a nice place to be, especially if you're in a really rough area of London and you've just finished a gig. No phone signal, no phone battery, no money and nowhere to stay – it's not great.'

One night, Ed found himself with nowhere to stay in the early hours in central London. He decided to bed down for the night rather than just aimlessly walk the streets. As he settled in he looked at around to see where he was and checked out the large building that loomed over the spot he had chosen. It was Buckingham Palace.

FIVE

THE NEXT BIG THING

Aged 17, Ed Sheeran was standing on the platform of Trefforest train station near Pontypridd in South Wales with his trusty Martin guitar and a small rucksack. Even for someone as well travelled as Ed, this was somewhere new. He was there to meet the Welsh singer-songwriter Amy Wadge. 'When I first picked him up from the train station I thought, "What on earth will we have in common?"' Wadge later told the website Wales Online. 'But he was incredibly passionate about music.'

This musical blind date had been arranged by Ed's management and Wadge's publishers. Like his work with Jake Gosling, the aim once again was to expand Ed's musical horizons and hone his songwriting skills. Amy was a seasoned singer-songwriter and experienced performer – there was talk at one stage of her replacing Cerys Matthews as lead singer of indie band Catatonia – but success had never fully come her way. In her early thirties and with her first child on the way, Wadge seemed to have accepted that the days of 'chasing a deal and mega stardom' were over. She'd recently signed a new publishing deal and part of the agreement was for her to work with new, unsigned talent. The first person she was sent under the arrangement was Ed Sheeran. After picking him up from the station, she took him back to her house at Church Village and Ed got out his small-scale guitar. 'He sat in the kitchen and played his track, "You Need Me, I Don't Need You",' Wadge later said. 'I kept running into the room and saying to my husband Alun, "Oh my God, this boy is unbelievable."'

Amy was expecting the songwriting session with Sheeran to produce one or two decent songs. She later recalled how she and Ed wrote nine songs over the next two days. 'I can't imagine there will be many times in my life that I will meet someone so incredibly gifted,' she later revealed to BBC Wales. 'To be honest I spent much of the next few days running in from my studio in the garden to tell my husband how sure I was that he was going to make me a millionaire.'

Ed and Amy agreed keep in touch after the session as she took him back to the train station: 'I remember saying to him, "Enjoy your life now because it's going to get crazy."'

After his trip to the Welsh countryside he returned to his relentless gigging schedule. For Ed, gigging seemed almost like a compulsion. His desire to perform live had developed a competitive edge – if he was going to play gigs, he was going to play more gigs than anyone else: 'I gigged pretty much every day,' he told the *Daily Mail*. 'My dad cut this article out about James Morrison. He said, "Look, this dude did 200 gigs in a year. He got the experience and then he got signed." My dad's attitude is to take someone you admire and not so much copy them as take their work ethic and do it twice as much.'

But Ed's enthusiasm for gigging would be sorely tested. Sometimes he would play to tiny huddles of people in small clubs. Sometimes, he'd play to no one. 'At certain points, if there's no one there and you're playing to a sound engineer, I did feel like giving up,' he told *Q* magazine. 'But I think it makes you a stronger person when you carry on.'

As well as his own solo gigs, Ed became a seasoned supporting artist. He supported his beloved Nizlopi and also appeared as an opening act for Noisettes, Jay Sean and Australian singer-songwriter Gabriella Cilmi, who Ed namechecks on 'You Need Me, I Don't Need You'. 'It's fantastic to do,' he told *IP1* about opening for other acts. 'It gets you out to a completely new audience who have never heard of you, so it's amazing to play to 400 strangers.'

He also joined a summertime package tour organised by promoters IK:TOMS that featured a rolling and ever-changing band of musical performers. Alongside Ed they included flamboyant singer and guitarist Tallulah Rendall, acoustic folk singer Stephen Long, electropop artist Grizla and hypnotic, low-key folkie Samantha Whates. The tour visited London, York, Manchester, Worcester and three nights in Edinburgh. It was a blur of beer, curry, late nights, early starts and long drives. Ed blogged about the tour at the time, not something he was in the habit of doing, and brought the experience to life in all its weird glory. 'All the sets were tight, and great to watch,' he wrote. 'Stephen was sporting his tour hat, which I fell in love with. I did my set at about 12ish to a lively audience, and a drunken man who was convinced I was Prince Harry, so that was an interesting experience!

'It's very hard for me to say how much I loved everyone on the tour,' he added as some of the acts came and went. 'It was just weird to say goodbye. In fact, no one really said goodbye, it was more of a mutual respect and a sorta, You know I love you, and I'll see you soon anyway, so it was very relaxed and cool. But all of the guys on tour were amazing, and I can't wait to play with them again.' Ed enjoyed himself so much he played for the same promoters at their Wired Festival in September. In fact he got so carried away at the gig he stripped off his shirt and played one song topless.

Ed also heeded some advice given to him by his music teacher Richard Hanley. 'Gentle guidance' is how Hanley describes it. 'Here's a competition – why don't you enter it? Why don't you apply?' He entered the 2008 Next Big Thing talent competition run by the *Norwich Evening News* and community radio station Future Radio. Previous winners of the competition had been The Kabeedies, Rosalita, Le Tetsuo and The Pistolas. None are household names but it didn't put Ed off from entering. In the end he beat off five other acts to win the competition: Rigo Jancsi, i am error, Adele Swallow, Killamonjambo and The Moo. Despite his win, Ed – ever the perfectionist – was unhappy with his performance. 'It wasn't the best show because as soon as I got on-stage, I snapped a lot of strings and had to ad-lib a bit,' he told BBC Norfolk after the gig. 'From that point on I didn't enjoy it as much because I was panicking, but it was a really fantastic thing to do and it was a surprise to win it. It's always really good promotion for yourself even if you don't win. It's a win-win situation.'

As he came offstage, Ed was collared by a reporter from the *Norwich Evening News*: 'This is a huge thing for me and I just can't believe I have won, especially after it all went so wrong with four strings breaking. I never normally break strings. I know it is a cheesy thing to say but everybody should be the winner tonight, they are all the next big things. I love performing and the atmosphere that comes with it. Even on Sunday night I enjoyed it despite the fact that everything went wrong and I thought the crowd would hate me.'

His prize for winning the competition included £250 in cash, studio time at Norwich's Future Studios, business advice and £750 worth of gear from music instrument company PMT. It's believed Ed took the opportunity to upgrade his road-worn Backpacker guitar in a move that would give his live work a distinctive look. He got a LX1E Little Martin – essentially a travel guitar that is built to a shorter scale than a normal sized guitar, perfect if you are travelling from gig to gig as Sheeran was doing. It's not a fantastically expensive instrument and will set you back just under £400, but as well as the sound, the Martin had other, more practical attractions for Ed: 'Going on trains, sleeping on sofas, playing around the country, you can fit a lot in the guitar's case,' he told *Total Guitar* magazine. 'And in the little pouch you can have your toothbrush and toothpaste and phone chargers. So it was my suitcase with a guitar in it and that was very convenient.'

Ed would remain stubbornly loyal to Martin – he's now an 'ambassador' for the company. He would eventually own an entire set of the Little Martin guitars, giving each a name – Nigel, Cyril, Felix and Lloyd – and imprinting them with a symbol that was to become his trademark: a cat's paw. Another piece of the Sheeran look and sound was in place.

Not long after the Next Big Thing win it was reported that Ed had signed a deal to release a single with Island Records, part of the Universal Music Group and home to acts as varied as Bob Marley and McFly. John Martyn had also been signed to Island. 'It was a big surprise. I didn't think anything like that would come this quickly,' Ed told the BBC at the time.

As late as February 2010 this release was still being reported as imminent, with the song he wrote with Jake Gosling when he was 16, 'The City', being named as the chosen single. Ed insisted that the agreement didn't affect his standing as being an independent artist – in fact he seemed positively cool about the whole idea. 'I'm not signed although I have a single coming out with Island Records, but that's more of a distribution deal,' he told the BIYL website in 2009. 'That's quite exciting, should get me some press and attention.'

Perhaps Ed's apparent lack of excitement about the deal stemmed from a personal plan he'd concocted and was about to put into action. It was a plan that he believed would get him what he wanted: a full-on record deal, but one that he could sign on his own terms.

* * *

Towards the end of 2009, Ed was asked by a reporter from *IP1* what his ambitions were for the coming year and beyond. 'There are lots of milestones along the way that would be great to achieve,' he replied. 'Headline a major festival, go platinum and play on Jools Holland.' Ed clearly had it all planned out but despite all the hard work, he had so far failed to secure a full record deal.

He seemed resigned to the fact that he would remain, for the time being, independent. It was almost like his desire – near-desperation – for a deal was putting record companies off: 'I think it helps if you kind of give up for a while,' he explained to UTOMusic. 'It's like with girls. If you stop showing interest in a girl, chances are she'll start showing interest in you. I found that with the record companies. When I was 16 I was like, Look at me, I'm a singer song-writer, I'm young. But none of them were on it. So I thought, OK, that's cool. I'm going to go away, do all my independent stuff. I'm going to build it up and do it independently. But I never ruled out the possibility that I might get offered a deal one day and it might be good and it might be a chance to push my music further.'

Ed's plan was to lay out his musical talents in a series of EPs featuring all the musical bases that he covered. The releases would touch on folk and indie, highlight his strengths as a live performer and feature his growing interest in grime and rap. 'There was a time when I was holding my songs back and being like, I'll wait until I'm signed and I can put an album out,' he explained to *Q* magazine. 'But after a while I thought, Fuck it, I'll just release EPs. Because the more music fans have on their iPod, the more of a fan they become. I put a five-point plan together of doing indie EPs.'

For such an 'organic' artist, there was something almost coolly cynical about Sheeran's five-point plan. Like a military operation he planned it out in almost forensic detail: 'I said, I'll create hype by making five EPs,' he told MTV. 'I'll make an indie one, a singer-songwriter one, a folk one, a live one and a collaborations one. And once those five are done, I would have probably built up enough hype to get signed.'

These EPs – added to his already impressive back catalogue of self-released material – would show any record company his full width and breadth as an artist. It would create a body of work that would act as a CV – the ultimate musical calling card. 'You can't understand who

Ed Sheeran is unless you listen to all of them,' he declared to OTUmusic.

Ed reconnected with producer Jake Gosling who he'd first met aged 16. Gosling now had a reputation as a rap producer and re-mixer. The stage was set for a full-on folk/urban fusion. 'He loves urban music – he loved Wiley and all the rappers I'd worked with,' Gosling later told *Sound on Sound*. 'But I also love folk, so we connected on a musical level straight away. It was a perfect fusion of the two together, really. We were trying to create something new.'

The result was the *You Need Me* EP, the first of five mission statements from Sheeran, all produced by Gosling and all designed to act as a wake-up call to record company executives. The songs on the EP almost fit together as a novella, telling Ed's story so far. 'So' seems to address the slightly shadowy figure of his girlfriend Alice, as Ed prepares to move away from the place and the girl he loves to pursue his dream of making it. It's a strange mix of acoustica and almost drum 'n' bass – the ideal combination of Sheeran and Gosling's sensibilities. 'The City' sees Ed and Jake sharing a writing credit on the song they had created when they first met when Sheeran moved to London aged 16 – which is exactly what the song is about. Lyrically it's an unsurprisingly naive take on a young man arriving in a city that 'never sleeps'; it has loops, Nizlopi bass slaps and slides, beats and strings – it's a little overcooked compared to the buzz and energy of Sheeran performing it with his loop pedal, building the song layer by layer. Here the energy of London is softened by a little too much syrup.

All the whistles and bells are put aside on 'Sunburn', an out-and-out Alice song that is just Ed, guitar and a cello. He's trying to recapture what he had, a relationship before it was spoiled by distance and distractions, and the song is all the better for the things that have been left off it. 'Be Like You' has all the summery chords and jazzy beats for a day at the beach – perhaps Brighton, which is name checked in the lyrics. One repeated section in the song – where Ed sings about popping on a dress and changing his eating habits – seems to have been drafted in from another tune, but it's beautifully sung by Sheeran.

The EP's title track would become one of Ed's most familiar songs, but the version here is Sheeran in Nizlopi mode with its shuffling drums and double bass slides. The looping outro section as Ed's voice doubles and triples into multiple layers is when the song really comes alive. Much would be written about 'You Need Me, I Don't Need You' being Ed's statement of dissatisfaction over his treatment by the industry at the time, but he'd been working on the song since he was 15, adding to it bit by bit. 'It's directed at a few people at once,' he later told the BBC's *Breakfast News*. 'The song's about my view on the industry at the time I got into it.'

Ed would later say that he'd been told not to rap, not to loop, to sing more like James Blunt and even to dye his hair blond. 'I've only got a few unique selling points and red hair is a big unique selling point. I'd never get rid of it,' he told the *Daily Record*. Ironically, he says he was also advised not to sing the song 'You Need Me, I Don't Need You' itself. Trouble was clearly brewing. 'When I got into the music industry, their view was that anything that had been successful before, use the same blueprint over and over again until it doesn't work any more,' he told the FaceCulture video channel. 'So, someone like James Blunt who sold 13 million records had a unique selling point. That's why he sold 13 million records. So the industry thing is let's get 30 kids with acoustic guitars who can sing some sort of love songs and release them. To be successful you have to have a unique selling point, so to copy someone else's blueprint isn't going to work. That's what the song is about.'

Some newer fans – perhaps unfamiliar with his older recordings – seemed slightly put out by the presence of a full band on the EP, as if it were a betrayal of his looping, improvisational live show. '"You Need Me" was full band and not a lot of people were keen on that,' he later told the Soulside Funk website. 'They were sort of like, Oh I don't know what you were trying to go for there because you should be a loop pedal person.'

That aside, the young singer now had an altogether slicker product to sell at his gigs and he and Gosling entered into an unusual arrangement to fund the remaining four EPs he planned to release. Each time he sold enough to generate £1,000 he would give the money to Gosling as a nominal fee to cover studio time for the next release. Gosling's time and efforts came free. 'The only way he lived was through selling his EPs,' Gosling later explained to music journalist Tom Doyle. 'Because I believed in what he was doing, I was like, Well look, if you can cover my cost on the studio, I won't recharge you, 'cause I love what you're doing. He'd get a couple of thousand printed up and just sell them at gigs everywhere he went. If he made 30 quid or 40 quid, he was over the moon about it.'

Among the many gigs that Ed played, one definitely stood out: a return visit to Framlingham and Thomas Mills High School. 'He came back to the school to perform at the charity concert the sixth formers organised,' recalls head of music Richard Hanley. 'It was his old year group's turn to organise the concert and they were still in touch with him. He came along and didn't bat an eyelid – he slotted in as if he hadn't been away.'

The relentless gigging continued and Ed sailed over James Morrison's tally of 200 performances. He collected the great swathe of train tickets he generated travelling around the country and kept them in an old wallet given to him by his dad. 'There are about four hundred,' he told BBC Blast about the symbolism of the tickets and the wallet. 'I have a saying that goes, If you don't know where you have been, you don't know where you are going.'

Sheeran secured a support slot with Just Jack – otherwise known as musician Jack Allsopp – thanks to a bit of good fortune. Things seemed to be going in his direction at last. 'The Just Jack tour wouldn't have come about if I didn't move above a pub where the guy that ran the night was friends with Just Jack,' he told Soulside Funk. 'It all fitted together.'

Ed would cite the show he played on the tour at the Shepherd's Bush Empire as one of his favourite gigs ever. On the tour he stood in the venue entrances selling the copies of his new CD to gig goers. He sold 'a few' which gave him enough to fund the recording of another EP. Again produced by Jake Gosling, the *Loose Change* EP was the widest palette yet for Ed's musical tastes. 'Songwriting wise I was trying to write something different, without being love songs,' he said. 'There's two love songs on there but I think they're quite a different theme of love – not, I love you ... but You buy me chips and cheese. I tried to go for different themes.'

Slightly stung by the negative reaction to the full band sound on his last release, Ed decided to change direction this time around: 'I also wanted to do something completely different production-wise to the last EP. So with this EP I was just sort of saying, I'm going to do something different as well this time. I'm not going to do what they want me to do, so I did something with a hip hop producer and made a different sound. It's worked and people like it.'

The self-explanatory track 'Homeless' is a looped, easy on the ear song featuring that scatting, not-quite-rapping wordplay that was starting to become a trademark. The song is co-credited to Anna Krantz, a London-born singer-songwriter whose talent hadn't quite matched her profile, in the same way as Amy Wadge. The two singers may share the credit but the lyrics seem inspired by Ed's journey as he describes his itinerant, rootless lifestyle chasing his musical dream. In fact it was sparked by one particular night he spent under the stars at a very special address: '"Homeless" is about a time when I was outside Buckingham Palace just sleeping because I had nowhere to stay,' he told the Soulside Funk website. The song also features a central lyrical pun. This would be a developing trademark of Sheeran's and many of his later songs would feature a touch of wordplay at their heart. In this case the pun was that thanks to his quest for a musical career he was now 'home less' than he'd like to be. Boom boom...

'Little Bird' is a swift-paced 'I really, really like you a lot' song that has received a wider audience after word got round it was Harry Styles of One Direction's favourite song. 'Sofa', another song credited as co-written with Anna Krantz, couldn't be more Sheeranesque as he describes a lazy day indoors watching telly, drinking tea and having a cuddle on the settee. 'One Night' is the closest Sheeran has ever got to sexy. It features that reference to 'chips and cheese' and also has a line that would find itself displayed on banners at Ed's gigs – a line about turning cheeks the same colour as your hair. 'Firefly' is no more than guitar, wooden blocks and voices, and has the feel of the José González track 'Heartbeats', though its minimalism is fleshed out on a gentle dubstep remix available as an additional track. The EP also has a live studio version of 'The City', with Sheeran looping, strumming and beatboxing for all he's worth – a far better take on the song than the laid back recording on the *You Need Me* EP.

But the EP would be most notable for its first track: 'The

A Team', a song with a back story and a song that would continue to have several other lives outside the parameters of the *Loose Change* EP. 'I have a friend who works at a homeless shelter every Christmas,' Ed later told the Press Association. 'He asked me to go along one year and play some songs for the people there. I met a girl called Angel, who was this amazing girl who really stood out – mainly because she was the only girl in the shelter and everyone else was male.'

Ed took his guitar with him that day – he found out that Angel's favourite band was Guns N' Roses, so he played her his rendition of 'Sweet Child O' Mine'. The shelter in question was plastered with laminated signs proclaiming lists of things that 'guests' could or could not do – they were called 'Angel's Rules'. Angel, it transpired, had broken all of the shelter's rules from the first day she arrived. To help make her toe the line, staff had invited her to draw up the rules, in the hope that would make her stick to them. 'She was kind of like the police in the shelter,' Ed recalls. 'What she said went, but she was always breaking the rules so the guys running the shelter had to strike a deal with her to get her to behave. I learned a lot about Angel, the unfortunate ways she earned her money on the street, and the things she did with it when she had it – it was a very bleak story. I spent some time with her playing her favourite songs, and then wrote "The A Team" for her.'

The arrangement and backing for the song are simple and straightforward and the lyric features a typical Sheeran piece of wordplay: the 'A' of the team in question being

Class A drugs. The vocal, particularly towards the end of the song, sounds very much like Luke Concannon. 'The A Team' would be a song whose time would come. Meanwhile a similar trajectory would be set down for another, even older song, 'You Need Me, I Don't Need You'. In February 2010 Ed recorded a version of the song for a new online channel called SB.TV. The SB stands for Smokey Barz, the nickname of Jamal Edwards, the much-feted young entrepreneur who started the channel in the kitchen of his mum's house in Acton, west London. Edwards had a touch of showbiz about from an early age: he was a stage school kid appearing in productions of *Cats*, *Oliver Twist* and *Annie*. His mum is *X-Factor* semi-finalist Brenda Edwards. When Jamal received a video camera for Christmas in 2006 he began casting around for ideas of how to make money from it. 'I was always hoping to win £250 from *You've Been Framed*,' he told *Q* magazine in 2012. 'I would leave banana skins on the floor hoping people would slip on them. No one ever does. I swear, it only happens in films.'

Instead he turned to filming foxes and insects in his back garden before turning his lens onto grime MCs on his local estate. 'I posted clips onto YouTube and I was amazed to see the hits rack up. It was a rush.'

Edwards was able to quit his job at Top Shop as SB.TV developed from a YouTube channel to its own website. Their first big hit was the clip of Sheeran, the person he now describes as his 'best mate': 'There are many artists that I've discovered and tapped into early through the SB.TV platform but probably one of the most recognisable would be Ed Sheeran,' he recently told Channel 4. The two met over Twitter: 'It was quite random how I met Ed, I must have asked [on Twitter] what movies should I go and see at the cinema? Is *Precious* good? And he replied yes and I went to check his Twitter out and checked his music out. The following week I went to one of his gigs then the week after that I recorded the video, which is now the most viewed on SB.TV.'

Sheeran's take on the song recorded for SB.TV makes the version available on *Loose Change* sound like fairly tame stuff. The fact that you could see Ed building the track section by section with his loop pedal made the video all the more compelling. He was showing you the trick while performing the trick, but the trick was still spellbinding. During the performance he references 50 Cent's 'In Da Club' and 'Red' by Bristol reggae band Laid Blak – a hymn to the joys of smoking marijuana – effortlessly showing his urban credentials to the SB.TV audience. Edwards believes he knows why the Sheeran performance was such a hit: 'If an artist comes in with something new and fresh, everyone is going to love it. We just provide a platform for them to do something amazing.'

Four thousand people watched the performance in the first few days it was online – three weeks later 20,000 people had seen it. As well as generating new fans, the video also provided a platform for Sheeran to reach out to a very different audience. Many of the grime artists he'd admired since he was young – and always wanted to work with –

suddenly took notice of him: 'As soon as I did the SB.TV video they all started contacting me,' he told the Blatantly Blunt video channel.

With his most completely realised piece of music so far in the can, a more urban style developing and the beginnings of a real online buzz, anyone would be forgiven for thinking that things were finally going Sheeran's way. But despite this Ed was still dissatisfied with the way his career was developing. 'I'd been playing the same gigs with the same people in the same bars and clubs,' he told FaceCulture. 'I'd be doing the same things every single day. I'd wake up, go to the studio, finish in the studio, do a gig, stay up for a bit then repeat it, repeat it, repeat it. Two years on from moving to London I was still doing it and I was wondering if this was the right thing.'

An indication of Sheeran's hand-to-mouth existence at the time is demonstrated by this posting on his Facebook, with Ed offering his musical services to his fans: 'Organising house gigs now. If you would like one, please email.' Six people responded to Ed's offer to play live at their homes for cash.

He took drastic action. First he split from his management. He then took another of his risks – and this one would outdo them all. 'I was living in Wood Green on a dude's sofa and I just got stuck in a rut,' he later told Q magazine. 'His mate was a poet from Los Angeles and she was like, "Oh I'll hook you up with a gig there."'

On the strength of one gig booking, Ed decided to leave London and head to America. He gathered up the money he'd made selling his CDs and bought a ticket. 'I'm off to sunny Los Angeles for a month on Monday,' he posted online on 2 April 2010. 'Can't wait!'

SIX

RASTA
MAN TIME!

'Some people don't believe this story because it is kind of unbelievable,' Ed would tell the BBC when asked about his visit to Los Angeles, 'but it definitely happened...'

The 'kind of unbelievable' story of Ed Sheeran's trip to America would make a great film script. But no one would make it because of its implausibility: ginger British teenager buys a ticket to Los Angeles and gets discovered by A-list Hollywood actor. It's far-fetched to say the least. It has occasionally seemed to niggle Sheeran that there's a belief his first American gigs and his 'discovery' by actor Jamie Foxx were down to luck and not attributable to his usual stock in trade: hard work. 'I didn't step off the plane and get a cab to his [Foxx's] house,' he told *Q* magazine. 'I gigged around, saved up a lot of money, booked a flight to LA with no contacts and started doing gigs. But it was really cool just to be invited into that world and be accepted. It was really nice.'

The story goes like this: in the first week of April 2010, a few weeks after his 19th birthday, Ed went to America on the basis of one gig. The plan was to stay for a month. 'I have a poet friend in London I gig with called Beth and she's from LA,' he told the BBC. 'I said, "I'd like to go there and do some shows." So she booked one show – a poetry show – and I stayed at a friend's house while I was out there.'

Sheeran's first gig was at The Savoy Entertainment Centre in Inglewood and seems on the face of it like a wildly inappropriate affair . The club is situated, in Ed's words, in 'not one of the most savoury areas of LA'. The scenario has almost been presented like a scene from the Eminem movie *8 Mile*, where a young white rapper has to prove himself in front of a largely black crowd. In an interview with OTUmusic, Sheeran described playing at Inglewood to 'hood gangsters'. In fact, The Savoy describes itself as 'the premier choice for Los Angeles' beautiful and professional urban trendsetters'. It's a rather swanky place: 'We're in Inglewood, we're an R&B club, we're pretty popular – we're open to everybody but it's primarily African-Americans,' Savoy owner Jonathan De Veaux told me.

De Veaux also gave me his memories of Sheeran's first ever US gig: 'So you've got this little white kid who came in and just tore the house down. I knew he was special. When I heard him I knew he was going to be a star – if the right people heard him.'

Apart from the club's host, Ed Sheeran was the only white face in the room when he walked into The Savoy that night,. 'I fitted in like a charm,' he recalled to Q magazine. When he arrived he also realised he would be the only musician playing that evening. Everyone else would be performing comedy or poetry. 'You have to have a unique selling point,' he later told journalist Dan Davies. 'If I'm the only singer-songwriter with a guitar who goes into clubs in Inglewood and plays a gig, that's good. I'd rather be the only one who does it than be one of 200.'

Sheeran might not have been a great one for homework back in Suffolk, but he certainly did it before his first gig in America. Before the gig he asked around as to what the up and coming track in the area was or who the local heroes were. Armed with that information he took to the stage. The initial reaction was one of bafflement – he started his set with 'You Need Me, I Don't Need You' – then Ed dropped a few lines of a 'local' song into his set. 'They were very odd with me before I played. Then once I'd played they accepted me. I played mostly urban places. I don't think I did a gig to one white person while I was out there. I was playing in Inglewood where Snoop Dogg's from, so I learned a verse from "The Next Episode" [a 1999 single by Dr Dre that features Snoop Dogg] and dropped that. That seemed to go down well.'

Club owner Jonathan De Veaux says the audience that night didn't care that that Ed was so young, that he was a touch scruffy in his casual street clothes, or that he was a white performer: 'No cares about the colour. He's good. It's not about the look. The look doesn't matter. The look only matters if you don't have talent. He's a star. Even before he was a star... we *knew* he'd be a star. Ed's got that "comes around every 20 years" talent. There're no gimmicks, it's just straight talent.'

Ever the entrepreneur, Ed also had some CDs and his trusty rucksack with him that night. He made about $200 from the Savoy audience. More importantly, it kicked off a series of events that would contribute hugely to Sheeran's success. It would also provide him with a highly marketable 'back story' that would give him a tale to tell when he was being interviewed 10 times a day the following year.

Ed would later describe the reaction he got that night at The Savoy as 'the best response I'd got from any crowd'. One audience member in particular was impressed and approached him after the show: 'That night, there was a girl there who ran Jamie Foxx's open mic night and she invited me to play there three days later.'

Stand-up comic, actor, musician and all-round Renaissance man, Jamie Foxx was and is a huge presence in Los Angeles. The star of *Collateral* and *Dreamgirls* was already an Oscar-winning actor thanks to his performance as Ray Charles in the 2004 biopic *Ray*. By 2010 he'd expanded his already impressive media portfolio with his

Foxxhole music and comedy channel on satellite radio network Sirius and a club night of the same name at The Conga Room in Los Angeles.

Jonathan De Veaux: 'I'm the one who got [Ed] on the Jamie Foxx show at The Foxxhole [club night]. I called up some of Jamie Foxx's people and got him on the Jamie Foxx night at The Conga Room. I worked on them and got Ed on the show. I said, "You've got to get this guy on the show." So they put him on the show.'

The night Ed arrived at The Conga Room, there was concern among the club's management about Ed's age. Because of the strict age limit on drinking in the US – you have to be 21 and Ed was barely 19 – it was decided that the teenage singer should be kept out of sight. 'When we were at the Conga Room, we actually had a problem,' says Jonathan De Veaux. 'I had to talk to the manger – they wanted to put him somewhere. They were worried that he wasn't 21. They were worried that he could be running around the club drinking. He didn't drink then so it wasn't a problem. I sat with him and got him sodas until he went on. He rocked it. Everyone went crazy there too.'

Ed: 'When I played there [The Conga Room] it was the same reaction. Jamie's manager was there and told me that Jamie would love my stuff, so he asked me to come and perform on Jamie's radio show.'

The version of 'You Need Me, I Don't Need You' that Sheeran played on Jamie Foxx's radio show is frankly blistering. The song had become stretched and added to over the years as Ed improved as a performer. Foxx and his studio entourage were clearly impressed and they can be heard voicing their approval with a series of 'Ohs' and 'Wows' as Sheeran builds up a head of freestyling steam. By the second chorus, Foxx is singing along and Sheeran lets rip: similar to the SB.TV version of the song, he drops some lines from 50 Cent's 'In Da Club', much to Foxx's delight. He then MCs a superfast section from 'Red' by Laid Blak – as the song shifts gear, Ed shouts 'Rasta man time!' As a finale he shamelessly drops a little of Foxx's own track 'Winner' in for good measure.

Foxx was impressed. As Ed later told MTV: 'When I performed on Jamie's show, he gave me his number and told me he had a studio that he created for musicians like me and said whenever I wanna make music, I could come in and use it, free of charge. The last person he did that to was [US soul singer] Anthony Hamilton, which makes me feel quite special.'

Ed picked up more and more gigs as he went along. He estimated he played around 23 shows during his American trip – not bad for a month-long stay. The uninhibited American audiences seem to take to Sheeran instantly – he was able to work the crowds with ease, getting one side of the room to out-sing the other and inviting people up on stage to sing and rap with him. But it wasn't all work – Ed proved he could still party with the best of them: 'I was taken to this frat boy/cheerleader party at this really, really rich dude's house,' Ed later told SB.TV. 'I didn't know anyone at all. I pretty much stayed up for two days straight. Really fun.'

It was following blow-outs like this in America that Sheeran decided to stop drinking, particularly after getting drunk at a house party that was awash with free, sponsored booze. Back in the UK, Ed's intense gigging schedule meant that after show partying was always available to him – and it had begun to catch up with the teenager. 'I played everywhere,' he later told OTUmusic. 'I did 312[gigs] in 2009. That nearly killed me, though. The thing is that after nearly every gig I'd drink a lot. It wasn't good.'

Part of the problem was that back in Britain, Ed spent the majority of his time in and around licensed premises. That's where the gigs were. Ed's cousin Gordon Burns: 'He told me that when he played the pubs all that time, they didn't pay him in money, they paid him in drink. In the end he had to say, I'd better stop this. That's common sense shining through. He seems to know himself and know his own mind.'

'From the age of 16 I was getting smashed every single night,' Ed confessed to the internet TV channel and POP. 'I got to 19 and I was like, I've been doing this for quite a while, I should probably stop. It can't be good for me.'

It's unusually self-aware for someone barely old enough to legally drink to stop drinking, but Ed Sheeran's lifestyle was unlike most teenagers. 'I was having a bit of a rough time,' he told MTV. 'I was playing the same gigs over and over again, sleeping on the same sofas and drinking a lot. Boozing was affecting his ability to work. Quietly, with no fuss, he decided to become teetotal. 'I need to get into the right headspace,' he later told the *Daily Star*. 'Drinking is fun but cutting it out has made a difference to me wanting to get up early. I don't want to do anything to ruin my chances of being successful.'

Ed believed that another reason he stopped drinking was because it made him... annoying. 'The reason that I don't drink is, I turn into an idiot,' he explained in 2012 to the M&C website. 'I've inherited my dad's genes, I just tend to tell not funny jokes when I'm drunk. I've had my cider in the park episodes. I stopped drinking because you find yourself drinking a lot in this industry. If you stop drinking it's a positive thing.'

From now on, Ed would stick to his favourite childhood drink: Robinson's Peach Fruit & Barley. When he became famous Ed would add the drink to his rider and received a years' supply of the drink from Robinson's after his double win at the BRIT awards.

Meanwhile, back in Los Angeles, Ed had a date at Jamie Foxx's house, to take the actor up on his offer of his recording facilities. It must have been with a little trepidation that Sheeran made his way to Hidden Valley, northwest of Los Angeles and rang the doorbell of the Jamie Foxx's $10million mansion. 'It was really surreal,' Ed recalled in an interview with the *Daily Telegraph*, 'because I was involved in all these family events, like a cowboy-themed birthday party, and he'd be in boots and a cowboy hat and on a horse, and they had [R&B singer and producer] Raphael Sadiq as the house band.'

Ed recorded some tracks in Foxx's studio – the facilities were impressive, but it was the family atmosphere that impressed Ed the most. 'The fact that he had his mum, his daughters, his friends, his family, people who work on his TV show, all living in his house,' he told SBTV. 'A very family-orientated man and so chilled out about it. He'd be there at the piano with his daughter running around saying, "Ed man, get the guitar – let's jam." That's his life, then he goes off and does a film and then comes back.'

Jonathan Le Veaux says there was a genuine buzz around Ed during his short American trip – there was even talk of him staying longer. If he had, then things might have gone very differently for the teenager. 'He had a lot of people that were trying to introduce him to people. I tried to introduce him to as many people as I could. But I'm in the nightclub business; I'm not in the talent management business. Jamie Foxx's people really wanted him and I think Jamie's manager was like, Damn we never should have let him out of the house… we never should have let him go back to England! I never really wanted anything from him. I thought the kid was talented and I thought everyone should hear him. I'm happy for the kid.'

At Jamie Foxx's mansion, despite having 10 bedrooms, Ed inevitably found himself in his natural habitat: sleeping on the sofa in its recording studio. There, Ed spotted something that caught his eye: 'He has a big glass cabinet with all his awards,' he later told Q magazine, 'and it's like, fuck, he has an Oscar *and* a Grammy.'

* * *

Ed returned to Britain invigorated, teetotal, sporting a new tattoo and in possession of an amazing story that would come in very handy over the next few years. He found that things started to fall into place for him. His first gig when he returned was at The Bedford in Balham. Ed had played there in the past and was a regular gig-goer there. He liked the venue and the venue seemed to like him too.

Perhaps it was not a coincidence that his fortunes were on the up. His return from America also saw him sign up with a new management company. He joined Twenty-First Artists, home at the time to Sir Elton John, Lily Allen and the man Ed had once been told to sing more like: James Blunt. Sheeran came under the wing of Stuart Camp, who'd joined the company from Atlantic Records and who'd been heavily involved with James Blunt's career – he'd been nominated for a Music Week award for his work in marketing *Back to Bedlam*, Blunt's second album. Soon Ed had prestigious support slots lined up with the likes of Professor Green and Example, a world away from his folkie roots. Camp took his role as a mentor to Sheeran very seriously and it wasn't long before Ed's sofa-surfing came to an end. He settled on his manager's sofa, where he was to stay for some time. 'My manager Stuart acted as a father figure, gave me a home and a sofa and really helped me,' he told OTUmusic. 'Everything started to go right when I got him.'

When it came to sofas, Ed Sheeran was a connoisseur. Here was a young man who knew his settees. He reckoned that, after five years of sofa-surfing, he'd finally found his favourite. 'You know, I think Stuart, my manager's sofa is probably the best sofa! It's a really big, massive white sofa with a really, really deep curve in it so you just kind of sink into it, it's wicked!'

Ed continued with his five-point plan. While he'd been in America he'd managed to oversee the release of another EP, barely two months after the arrival of *Loose Change*. That EP had sold well – at the time he estimated it had shifted 3,000 physical copies and 8,000 on download – so the funds were quickly available to make another. The self-explanatory *Songs I Wrote With Amy* came from the Trefforest sessions with Amy Wadge two years earlier. The two had kept in touch and had collaborated on more songs. 'Ed asked me to do backing vocals on an EP he was doing at the time,' she explained to BBC Wales. 'I was heavily pregnant with my second child so couldn't travel. Ed carried on without me and the EP was released, and to my surprise he'd called it *Songs I Wrote With Amy*.'

The five songs on *Songs I Wrote With Amy* – all co-credited to Wadge – are polite, discreet adult offerings that seem aimed at a grown-up audience. In terms of his five-point plan, this is Ed's 'folk' EP. On 'Fall', Wadge mirrors Ed's vocals virtually word for word over a tasteful guitar, piano and brushes accompaniment. Wadge seems to bring the best out of Ed's singing and his voice sounds fuller, like he is stepping up to the mark in Wadge's more experienced presence. 'Fire Alarms' is summery and light with Wadge taking more of a back seat; it sounds like another 'Alice' song as he recalls dodging school with his love, while being worried that life is running away from him.

'Where We Land' sees Ed in familiar Damien Rice territory – his opening line is very O-esque – and again Wadge is on hand to shadow Sheeran's vocal lines. It's a very traditional sounding song to the extent that it sounds like a cover version of a standard. Lyrically it has a real sense of Rice about it too, as Ed struggles to work out how he feels about someone, before shrugging his shoulders and deciding to just see how things pan out. It's short, sweet and the best track here.

'Cold Coffee' is a grown-up, 'morning after the night before' song and is the most commercial offering on the EP – it sounds like it's crying out to be playlisted by Radio 2. In a sense this is one of the problems with some of the tracks on offer – how many teenage performers would aspire to such a 'middle of the road' sound? The final track 'She' is largely Sheeran's vocals on his own, though Wadge is there on the chorus. It features a typically Sheeran-style bit of punmanship, as he describes his love as being like paperwork, 'but harder to read'. Wadge in particular seemed tickled by this bit of wordplay: 'He was 17 when we wrote "She" and he came up with those words,' she told BBC Wales. 'I knew right then he was incredibly special.'

Despite the slightly safe sound of the EP, the most startling thing about the collection is that these world-weary songs of mornings after, indecision and regret were co-written by a 17-year-old. For her part, Amy Wadge seems more than grateful for her time with Ed Sheeran, and Ed's future success meant that Wadge's stock would rise considerably over the coming years. 'A track from *Songs I Wrote With Amy* was recently featured on an episode of [US comedy series] *Cougar Town* and is the b-side to the American release of "The A Team",' she told the BBC in 2011. 'All of a sudden all the doors that were so tightly shut before have flown open and I am writing with some incredible new artists. It's the most exciting time in my career and I can do it all from the comfort of my own home.'

By now, Ed's EPs had begun to make a real dent in the iTunes chart, though there would be a slight identification problem that would confuse some fans. 'There is another dude on iTunes called Ed Sheeran,' he told BBC Nottingham. 'So if you hear a folky, warbling old guy that's him. That's not me. Some people have made that mistake and bought that, then contacted me and said, "Why didn't you tell us?"'

The 'other' Ed Sheeran's album was his 2006 offering *Songs of Life and Hope*. Anyone hearing the full-bodied, booming voice and countrified folk of this Ed would be hard pressed to confuse it with Ed Sheeran, hip hop folk singer. The confusion wasn't helped by many sites – including Amazon – stating that this *was* Ed Sheeran, hip hop folk singer. The misinformation continues to this day.

Meanwhile, Sheeran found that some friends had been busy while he'd been away and that his first 'proper' music video was ready to be uploaded. It was a track from *Loose Change* and in typical Sheeran style the video had been done on a tight budget: 'The video for "The A Team" was done for £20,' he later explained to *Q* magazine. 'I was living with this amazing actress and she had a friend [photographer Ruskin Kyle] who wanted to make a video for me. So I said, "Cool." I gave him "The A Team" and she said, "I'd love to play Angel." So we had a meeting and they said, "We need to buy a crack pipe and some fishnets." So I gave them £20. They went off for a week, they rang me once to go and do a cameo and they came back with the finished video.'

The simple, slightly literal video tells the tale of a homeless girl (played by Ed's friend Selina MacDonald) who turns to prostitution to get her off the streets, only to be killed by the drugs she decides to spend the money on. Sheeran appears briefly, buying a copy of *The Big Issue* from 'Angel' and stopping for a quick chat. The £20 video was uploaded to YouTube on 22 April 2010. So far it has had nearly 45 million views.

There's no happy ending in the video – and that seems

to reflect the real life story it was based on. In 2011 Sheeran returned to the shelter to find Angel: 'I went back and she wasn't there,' he told Q magazine. 'I don't know what's happened.'

SEVEN

WHY ON EARTH ARE YOU NOT SIGNED?

Ed's new management were clearly working hard on his behalf – he got his first ever paying gig. He received £50. Not bad for someone who had played more than 400 gigs for free. As far as he was concerned, playing for free was all part of the deal and he advised other budding musicians to follow his lead: 'With gigs, you don't get paid until you get to a certain level,' he told the website I Love Music. 'So just do as many as you can for free until you can get up to that level, because once you hit a certain level, when you've got a certain amount of gigs under your belt, you can demand higher fees because you've done it all for free. Just don't expect it to come easy, but do have fun whilst doing it.'

Other new career developments quickly began to take

shape: discussions began for Ed to play some gigs with a full band and his touring schedule took on a whole new dimension with gigs in Canada lined up and two full-on tours supporting dance rapper Example.

Money was still tight, but a young man still has to eat. While on tour with Example, Ed hit on a plan that he hoped would fill his belly on the road for nothing. The internet was buzzing with talk of the Nando's Black Card or the High Five as it's also known. It was claimed that the high street chicken chain's PR people had been giving out the cards to pop stars, actors and celebs in a canny marketing move. The cards qualified the lucky recipient to get free food for up to five people as often as you like for a year. Example already had one. Sheeran wanted one too and hit upon a plan. In the loading area behind the Waterfront venue in Norwich he and Example performed 'The Nando's Skank' on camera. The pair dance, sing and swear their way through a song extolling the virtues of peri-peri chicken and the card that could get Ed free access to it. When Ed drops in a bit of The Kings of Leon ('my tongue is on fire!') all concerned collapse with laughter. The video was uploaded to YouTube and soon caught the company's attention: 'Nando's have put the freestyle me and Mr Example did on their Facebook page,' he wrote online. 'Love it!' Ed got his Nando's card. 'It was just a YouTube video, a ploy to get a black card,' Ed later explained to The Red Room video channel. 'And it worked. I'm thinking of doing "The Pizza Express Skank" soon, just so I can get free Calabrese, Coca Cola, doughballs with Nutella.'

Example's brand of radio-friendly dance anthems had provided him with some big hits like 'Won't Go Quietly', 'Kickstarts' and 'Last Ones Standing' over the previous year. He had handpicked Ed to support him on the tour: 'I first saw Ed Sheeran on SB.TV and I was amazed at how unique he was. You just can't pigeonhole him. I asked him to support me on both of my headline tours.'

Not all of Example's audiences on the tour were as enthusiastic when Ed walked out on stage with his little guitar. 'I was doing a gig supporting Example at Exeter and I got a bottle chucked at my head as I walked on stage,' he later told the BBC. 'I thought, Right, this is going to be a challenge. By the end of it I had them all singing along, buying CDs and t-shirts. That's what you have to learn, how to do that.'

Meanwhile, Ed was coming up with new ways of generating cash at his merchandising stall. As well as CDs there were now t-shirts and hoodies bearing his paw-print insignia, plus some new items: jewellery made by his mum Imogen. 'I started making jewellery after the funding was cut for a youth arts programme I was working for,' she told the EADT website. 'It needs a good eye and a bit of dexterity and I started to work on some of my own designs. I made some liquorice allsorts bracelets for Ed to start with and they went down very well.'

As well as the jewellery based on sweets and food, Imogen also started to make more discreet pieces that could be sold at her husband John's art talks: 'I've got two themes to my jewellery – fun and funky, which is the pieces I make for Ed, and then grown-up and gorgeous. It's lovely to be doing it for John and Ed and it's really a labour of love. My motto for the jewellery is: handmade with love. Everything I make is a one-off – so no one else will have one of them.'

Rupert Grint and Jessie J would soon be spotted wearing Imogen's jewellery, but the big breakthrough would come the following year when the Duchess of Cambridge was spotted wearing a Smartie-inspired bracelet during a high-profile charity event in Ipswich. The £10 pieces were designed to raise money for the East Anglia Children's Hospice. Ed took to Twitter to mark the moment, writing: 'Big up Kate Middleton, who is wearing some of my mum's homemade jewellery!'

The majority of Ed's income was still from selling his CDs, and part four of his five-point EP came in the shape of the *Live at The Bedford* EP. The CD (and DVD in early editions) had a simple purpose: to showcase Sheeran's abilities as a live performer. Ed had become a seasoned supporting act for other artists; sometimes, as with the bottle throwers on the Example tour, it had been a challenge. Now it was time for Ed to start his career as a headliner. A live EP would be the perfect calling card.

During the summer, in between support slots with rapper Professor Green and recording sessions for his next EP, he started to prepare for the full band show that could feature on the recording – he played his first gig with the band at the Rhythm Factory in Shoreditch, east London in June. Ed asked people who had subscribed to his Facebook page what kind of live experience they'd like. Some said they

Thomas Mills High School

Christmas Concert

Tuesday 18th December 2007

1st Orc...

Flute...
Director: D...

Strin...
Soloists...
Cor...

Solo...

B...
Direc...

Y...
Direc...

So...

D...

INTERVAL Mince Pies and Mulled Wine to be served in the Sports Hall

2nd Half

Orchestra Violin: Ella Virr	The Lark Ascending	Vaughan Williams
Orchestra	The Radio Four Theme	Fritz Speigel
Solo: Emily Winter Piano	Fantasy in D minor	Mozart
Wind Band Solo: Vee Singleton	The Typewriter	Anderson
Samba Group Director: Laura Scott	Samba!	
Solo: Dan Chapman	Old Devil Moon	arr. Cullum
Jazz Group Director: David Abbott	Hark the Herald Angels Swing	F Mendelssohn arr. Ed Bell
	Pick up the Pieces	Roger Bell and Hamish Stuart arr. D Abbott
Senior Choir Director: Laura Scott	Medley from Guys and dolls	Frank Loesser arr. Mac Huff
Jazz Trio	So What!	Miles Davis
Solo: Ed Sheeran	Song from latest album	
Grand Finale	Way back into Love	Schlesinger arr. Hanley & Hanley
Playout	Sleigh Ride	Anderson

Retiring Collection in aid of Tercentenary Fund. Thank you.

Above: A programme for one of Ed's early gigs at his school in Framlingham.

© *Thomas Mills High Schoo...*

Left: Gary Dunne, who taught Ed the 'looping' guitar style that's a vital part of his sound.

© *Gary Dunn...*

Right: Ed on stage at The Enterprise, London in February 2008.

Left: Ed in Camden, London, in early 2008.   © *Getty Images*

Left: A triumphant headlining appearance at Shepherd's Bush Empire in October 2011.

Right: Sheeran with Example – co-author of the 'Nando's Skank' – at the *Q* awards in October 2011. Ed was named best breakthrough artist.

© *Getty Images*

Above: The Brits were announced with help from Jessie J, Harvey Alexander-Sule and Jordan Stephens from Rizzle Kicks flanking Ed Sheeran and Professor Green.

Below: Ed with Tony Moore of The Bedford in Balham, the venue used for recording his live EP.

© *Getty Images*

In 2012 Ed Sheeran won the Ivor Novello award for 'The A Team', the year's best song musically and lyrically.

Sheeran performing for the Queen's Jubilee in June 2012 and meeting Her Majesty with Kylie Minogue.

Sheeran with young fans at RockNess in June 2012. © *Anna Robb and Lachlan Jardine Munro*

wanted to hear Ed on his own with just his guitar and his loop pedal. Others said they'd fancy hearing him play with a full band. Ever the people pleaser, perhaps Ed didn't want to risk upsetting anyone, so he did a bit of both.

On Sunday 17 October 2010, Ed performed at The Bedford in Balham, southwest London – the gig was filmed and recorded for his first live EP. 'I'm not going to play with a band again for a long time,' he wrote online, 'so come along and enjoy the new shit.'

The Bedford is one of London's largest pubs and has a 150-year-old theatre at the rear. The venue also has a history of championing artists on the lower rungs of the ladder: 'Primarily our shows are free and we're generally working with artists who can't sell a ticket,' Tony Moore, director of music, art and development at The Bedford told me. 'Over ten years we've had Paolo Nutini, James Morrison, Amy Macdonald, Newton Faulkner and Seth Lakeman come along at the beginning of their careers – when they didn't have an audience and they were learning their stagecraft – and we have been a part of what they do.'

Ed was a regular at The Bedford – as a punter as well as a performer. 'Ed's journey had crossed with many artists who'd played at The Bedford,' Moore explained. 'I know he'd come down and supported other performers and he was really good friends with Luke Concannon from Nizlopi, who we'd championed. Ed had worked closely with Nizlopi and Ed was one of these musicians who've always been dedicated to improving and learning. I see thousands and thousands of performers coming through.

You get an instinct for an act that could really take off. Ed was always great – you could see him growing and developing every time he came back to the venue. It was always a pleasure to have Ed on our stage.'

The tracks on Ed's EP *Live at the Bedford* are largely familiar ones – it's the way that many of the songs are played that delivers the surprises. It was as if Ed was trying to make a further point: I can collaborate with other musicians as well as being a one-man band. Sheeran plays alongside a band featuring Neal Flynn on bass, Adrian Brudney on guitar, Louis Essuman on keyboards, backing singer Sophie Pringle and Ash Roye on drums.

The band members – known as The Remedies – were all part of the Music is Remedy collective, which runs music events across London, providing musical backing for soul singers, poets and hip-hop MCs. Their contribution can be heard straight away on *Live at the Bedford* on 'The A Team' – it's subtly filled out with finger-picking guitar, brushes, backing vocals and a little bit of tooty – some might say unnecessary – sax. Sheeran's take on the song is tougher than previous versions – he almost gasps for breath as the track and the vocal builds. 'Homeless' is given the same treatment – it's not exactly rocking out but there's a sense of Sheeran using it as a way of saying, I'm not just all sensitive you know, I can let rip too. It also features Ed leading an audience sing-song for the song's outro. 'The City' is Ed on more family looping territory before the full band kicks in, giving the song that big city urgency that the original version lacked. But again, ease off on the sax guys. 'Fall' is the most low-key track on offer and sees Ed accompanied by young Essex singer Leddra Chapman standing in for Amy Wadge.

'Wake Me Up' is the fresh track here – written while Sheeran was the worse for wear in Los Angeles – and is his most explicitly Alice song. It's performed with Ed accompanying himself on guitar – his impassioned vocal elicits whoops of delight from the Bedford crowd – and it's the best track on the EP. Things are rounded off with a ten-minute version of 'You Need Me, I Don't Need You', a marathon blast of loops and live band that provides the aggressive thump to match the anger of the lyrics. As he's done in the past, Sheeran references 50 Cent and Laid Blak but a big chunk of the running time is given to a call-and-response sing-song with the audience and a rap from guest artist Random Impulse, who'd also appear on Sheeran's *No 5 Collaborations*. As an encore – it doesn't appear on the CD – Ed pulled his old folkie trick, took a couple of chairs into the audience and sang without amplification, performing 'Sunburn' and 'She' with Leddra Chapman.

Tony Moore: 'I know the night that Ed did the show at The Bedford was the most packed we'd ever had in the theatre. Ed's agent said that night was a critical night, because everyone who was involved with Ed or watching his progress suddenly realised that here was an artist who could fill a space with 300 people and make them part of an experience... and that is a rare thing. All of those indicators that we had been seeing with Ed over the few years of him coming here and performing culminated in this amazing night. It was a catalyst that proved what he could do. For an unsigned artist, no one has filled that room before to that capacity. We were thrilled for him. You and I are talking about this event now but at the time, no one knew what was going to happen. Until it happened.'

The show was reviewed by the Soulside Funk website: 'The whole night he had the crowd in his hands, near silence during the slow songs and riotous cheering during the lively ones,' the review said. 'He was performing like a seasoned pro many years his senior. Consistency is a difficult thing to achieve, and Ed certainly has a consistently high standard for his shows which is an incredible achievement, especially for someone who is still doing it all on his own. Earlier on someone yelled out, "Why on earth are you not signed?" It was almost like pantomime when someone else (probably his manager) shouted, "Blame his management!" All jokes aside, if the curtains come down on 2011 and Mr. Sheeran does not have a record contract to his name, it will make a complete mockery of the "so called" British music industry. I'm still rooting for the good guy with scruffy ginger hair!'

Released in November, *Live at the Bedford* was a modest success compared to the kind of sales that were just around the corner. However, Ed was thrilled by the project and its chart performance. 'It's been received really well and ended up charting at 130 in the national charts and Number 4 in the singer-songwriter charts,' he told BBC Suffolk at the time. 'It's mental. I didn't even put any backing into it – I just put it online. I think it's because I gave the people what they wanted. A year ago I wasn't getting as much attention as I am now. I'm grateful to every person who comes to a gig and talks to me. They're really cool people and I'm in a happy situation at the moment.'

Ed Sheeran was breaking through. People were staring to recognise him: 'It's hard *not* to get recognised with having bright ginger hair and having a guitar on your back,' he told OTUmusic. 'With me not living anywhere I always have a guitar on my back and a rucksack. Even if you don't know who I am ... *you know who I am*. It's like, There's that ginger kid that plays guitar. That happens a lot. Some people think I'm someone else. Some people call me Ben Sherman. Or Ed Sherrington. Or Sherman Sherwin. It's not got to the point where everyone knows who I am, people just know there's a ginger out there with a guitar.'

During the summer of 2010, Ed had returned to Sticky Studios to start work on the final instalment of his five-part run of independent EPs. The exposure he had received through his appearance on SB.TV opened him up to a whole new world of acts that now wanted to work with him. It would serve a key purpose, that of establishing Sheeran as a credible, modern artist, perhaps dampening down those concerns that he might be a bit 'Radio 2' for a younger audience.

Around this time a genuine buzz was hovering around Sheeran's work and there's a sense that the EP was done while he was still in a position to be able to do what he wanted to do as an independent artist. If he were to do it after he'd signed it might look fake. 'If I were to do a collaborations album with a label, the label will put thei input into it, and if it becomes huge, then everyone will say grime is the big thing at the moment,' he explained to MTV. 'So it will be like the label has taken this white singer-songwriter and stuck him with a bunch of grime MCs to get him hype. And I actually wanted to prove I have a serious love for the music and I really respect the MCs I'm working with. I've been listening to them years before they got hype and also I proved I could do it myself. I contacted all the MCs myself and personally asked them to be on the project. There was no fabrication. It was all very organic. So therefore, why not just keep it all grassroots? I don't give a shit if I don't sell 30,000 copies. The whole point of this was to create something that would be remembered. It's never about the sales. This project is all about the music, so doing it independently was the best route.'

Jake Gosling was once again in the producer's chair for the project. 'The concept was put together from what he had been wanting to do for some time,' Gosling wrote in his blog, 'and get the rappers that he respected and admired to work with on one LP – or EP or whatever it is – there are many more artists he wanted to get on but... there's always part 2!!'

By now, Ed was earning a co-production credit alongside Gosling: 'People get mixed up with co-production nowadays,' Ed said. 'Production in hip hop means you make the track. Whereas production in my world means you tweak a few buttons and make it sound right. So I wasn't really sure how to credit it. Whether I was the producer because I did all the music or Jake was the producer because he did the real production. So... co-production.'

Jake Gosling: 'All tracks have been produced by me and with Ed's co-production vibe and all written by myself and Ed alongside the relevant rapper for each track. This is not Ed's main album, but a reflection of what he likes about music and sounds and lyrics without having the pressure from any labels or outside pressures before he embarks on his solo album for next year.'

The EP was named the *No.5 Collaborations Project* – as ever with Sheeran, even the title had a well thought-out purpose: 'It was kind of a full stop,' he told Blatantly Blunt TV. 'I did four EPs beforehand and my whole business plan was to do five EPs: an indie one, a singer-songwriter one, a folk one, a live one and then a collaborations EP. I was going to call it *Collaborations*, but if I called it *No.5* then people will slip back and check out the four others.'

The final roll call of grime artists and MCs to appear on the EP was: Devlin, Wiley, P Money, JME, Ghetts, Mikill Pane, Random Impulse, Sway, Wretch 32 and Dot Rotten. 'Lately' kicks things off, a brooding, atmospheric piece highlighted by a classic hip hop 'pling pling' riff and featuring an aggressive rap by Devlin, a Dagenham MC with connections to several other artists on *No.5*. It's a scat/sing affair from Sheeran as he delivers an update on his sofa-surfing insomniac lifestyle. 'You' showcases rapper and grime MC Wiley, with Ed initially taking a back seat, churning out an echoing John Martyn-style guitar riff before joining in with a chorus vocal that's pure Luke

Concannon. The track was a collaboration between two people who had never met. 'I've spoke to him on the phone a lot and I've done some vocals on tunes for him, but I've never met him,' Sheeran told SB.TV. 'That was the first tune we completed, so it was quite a good benchmark. But the mad thing is that everyone on the EP I hang out with on a friendship level now, so I really wanna meet Wiley just to tell him how great he is.'

'Family' matches Sheeran's bluesy wail with throbbing synth drones and P Money's super fast rap about his real-life recovery after a car crash. 'Radio' features low-key rhymes from north London rapper JME and some punning wordplay from Sheeran about his position as an outsider in the music industry. Like many of the tracks, it was specifically created with the artist in mind: 'Most of them are specifically tailored for the acts,' Sheeran said. 'Like, JME's very set in his opinions so I made him a track about not being played on the radio.'

'Little Lady' is instantly recognisable as the backing track to 'The A Team' and features Mikill Pane and a story rap that extends the tale of Angel in the original song in a more explicit, brutal manner. Pane was the least known of all the collaborations: 'He's called Justin,' Ed explained to OTUmusic. 'He just used to come to a lot of gigs and he stands out like a sore thumb. He's a huge tall bloke with (mimes big ears) and loads of tattoos and a cool dress sense and I got talking to him and he became a really good friend. Then I found out he could really, really spit [rhymes]. I was doing a gig in Old Street and I was staying on someone's sofa in Chalk Farm and he walked me back.'

As they walked they exchanged rhymes and Sheeran heard Pane rap a story that complemented his own from 'The A Team'. Ed got him into studio as soon as possible and replaced 'The A Team's verses with the new rap. It was recorded in one take. 'I was expecting people to hate it and, "You've ruined our favourite song blah blah blah." But no one's said a bad word. I had people like Just Jack texting me saying, "Who's Mikill Pane?" And Professor Green saying the best track on the EP's Mikill Pane.'

'Drown Me Out' – featuring east London grime rapper Ghetts – is a huge-scale piece with clattering drums, echoing guitars, multi-layered Eds on the chorus and machine-gun rhymes. 'Nightmares' has Ed on guitar loops and a hefty cast of MCs, rappers and musicians including Wretch 32 – it's as busy as it sounds. Final track 'Goodbye to You' features 1980s synth runs, lush backing from Ed, fuzztone guitar and a heartfelt rap from Dot Rotten. It's an 'everything but the kitchen sink' production from Jake Gosling to round off a remarkably diverse musical collection.

'Every single song was as musical as I could make it,' Ed explained to music writer Joseph Patterson. 'I really didn't wanna make any songs about girls. On the P Money track, he speaks about being in a car crash, so I wanted it to be a spiritual thing about being taken home. With the Dot Rotten one, it's about saying goodbye to someone, and he went really deep on it. With the Ghetts track, I really wanted to bring the old Ghetts back. I wanted to get him on a really grimey beat. Devlin is just so lyrical. With the JME track, we bought a bit of humour to the project. Every single song is so different and every MC I worked with on this project brings something totally new and completely fresh to the table.'

Wretch 32 agreed: 'Ed is the coolest guitarist I have met,' he told *The Sun*. 'He also has a grime artist work ethic. The scene has united to help promote his sick EP.'

The finished product created genuine buzz around Sheeran, and Radio 1 and 1Extra showed great interest in one track, 'Radio'. So it transpired that the song about not getting played on the radio... was the first one to get played on the radio. Ed was standing by ready to listen when Jo Wiley played 'Radio' on Radio 1 for the first time. 'That was quite a let-down actually,' Ed would later recall in an interview with radio station Baltimore 106.5. 'I was in the car with my girlfriend and she was dropping me off at the station. The song had just begun and I was like, Wicked – my song's on Radio 1 for the first time. She stopped at the station, turned the engine off and took the keys out. The radio cuts out and I'm like, Oh no! My first time on the radio and I hear ten seconds of it! She put the keys back in and we searched for the station again. By the time we get there, it's the last chord. A tiny bit disappointing, but still kinda cool.'

One thing wasn't quite clear to many people though: what kind of music was this? 'It's not really grime music,' Ed told SB.TV. 'It's more like singer-songwriter with some hip hop beats. Every MC came from a real approach; they took a bit of their heart out and put it on the track. That was them, not me. I just supplied the backing track and the chorus and the original concept. With the P Money song, all I did was make the chorus and do the beat and stuff. People gave me too much credit. People say I brought the best out of the MCs, but I think the MCs brought the best out of me. It was a collaborations project, it happened the way it should've done.'

Meanwhile Ed was getting closer and closer to signing a full record deal – he would have to get the collaborations project out swiftly if it was to be released while he was still an independent artist. Just before Christmas, Ed played a lunchtime gig at The Waterside in Norwich ahead of a sold-out evening show. He told the audience – many of them wearing t-shirts with Ed's paw print logo on them – that he'd agreed to sign with a record company a few days earlier. He wouldn't name the label, but he told reporters from BBC Norfolk: 'I'll be heading straight into the studio in the new year. I'm just really keen to make a good album.'

Ed's final EP as an independent was released in January 2011. Reviewers were bowled over by the combination of grime, loops and folk. 'For an artist on the precipice of mainstream recognition,' said Soul Culture, 'No.5 Collaborations Project is arguably the most anti-commercial project to emerge from someone at that level. Yet Ed Sheeran's ode to grime, dystopia and family is invigorating and powerful, which challenges the notions of what an artist of his genre (and appearance) should produce.'

Urban music blog Bangers and Smash said: 'Ed's *No.5 Collaborations Project* looks set to kick start a breakthrough year for an act that has the potential to cross the genre boundaries that have so often stifled a career. What this project has done in eight tracks is a remarkable achievement, with Ed's singer-songwriting skills acting as the perfect foil in letting some of grime's most notorious MCs bare their souls. What started as a collaborations project looks like being a turning point not only in Ed's career but hopefully opening a whole new audience to the homegrown ability of some of grime's legends and best kept secrets.'

Grime Daily – exactly the kind of website Sheeran was trying to get on board – said: 'What Ed Sheeran's album has done though, is lift grime up a couple of notches. It has raised the game, raised levels and raised the depth of grime. We all know, as grime fans, the music gives us a buzz – it's hype, it's for the raves and parties, but the tracks Ed has presented us with, presents grime artists on a different level. I'm going to throw it out there and say this album makes me want to call it "Grime'n'B", it's entirely different, and a step forward for unsigned artists and for grime.'

But it wasn't just the specialist websites and outlets that were taking notice – even *The Sun* was starting to get behind Sheeran: 'Wonderkid Ed Sheeran is fast becoming one of the UK urban scene's hottest properties,' the paper told its readers.

The EP began to sell, moving slowly but steadily up the iTunes chart. 'I woke up in the morning and it was at number 46,' he told Blatantly Blunt TV. 'I was like Number 46, sick, yeah, wicked! Number 46! And then I left it. Then I got a text saying it's Number 12. Then I checked it – it was Number 9 and it kept growing and growing and growing. Then it was Number 2. I don't really know how it happened. Everyone got into on Twitter and I think it was a bit of a snowball effect and people like Tinie [Tempah] and Pixie Lott and Rio Ferdinand, Tom Felton from *Harry Potter* tweeted about it. Twitter was the only contribution. That was the marketing plan.'

Ed's fan base was getting bigger and bigger – and ever more famous. 'I don't answer unknown [phone] numbers as a rule,' he told Access Hollywood, 'and this unknown number kept ringing me and ringing me. I probably had about seven missed calls from it. Then I had a text from my manager saying... pick up your fucking phone, it's Elton!' Before long, Ed would be having weekly chats about his career with Sir Elton John, particularly when Sheeran transferred to Elton's management company Rocket Management. 'He's very involved,' Ed told *The Sun*. 'It's always good to hear from Elton. He's a lovely guy and is very passionate about the music. He wants me to be huge all over the world, and I'm up for that too.'

The EP sat at Number 2 on iTunes, behind Rihanna. On 14 January, *The Sun*'s showbiz editor Gordon Smart – by now well and truly on the Sheeran bandwagon – went one further: 'I've been singing the praises of Ed Sheeran for some time now. So today I'm feeling a little smug that his debut EP, *No.5 Collaborations Project*, has rocketed to No 1 on the iTunes album chart. The singer-songwriter's inspired collection, which features duets with some of grime's top dogs including Wiley, Devlin and Ghetts, knocked Rihanna off the top spot in just two days. The eight-tracker has been released completely independently, funded by Ed himself and it's had a very small amount of radio play.' The headline over the article read: Sheeran – Labels Kicking Themselves.

Even Ed's plan to use *No.5* as a signpost to his previous EPs worked. As he predicted, *Loose Change*, *You Need Me* and *Songs I Wrote With Amy* all followed *No.5* into the charts. Ed Sheeran's bigger plan, though, was to release a series of EPs that showcased who he was and what he did – a showcase that any major label would be foolish to miss, because it was so convincing in its range and potential. 'A year ago when there was no hype, I said I'll create hype by making five EPs,' he stated in an interview with The Wrap Up website. 'I'll make an indie one, a singer-songwriter one, a folk one, a live one and a collaborations one. And once those five are done, I would have probably built up enough hype to get signed.'

As *No.5 Collaborations Project* sat at the top of the charts, it was announced that Ed Sheeran had signed a major record deal. 'The EP has hit the iTunes charts with virtually no radio play, released independently with no label backing. We've got grime artists high up in the chart with the backing and support of our fan base. A guy from one of the big labels told me he was gutted they didn't sign me two years ago when they had the chance,' Ed told *The Sun*. 'Now I'm signing with Atlantic.'

EIGHT

POSITIVE

The Station pub in Framlingham is more used to hosting birthday parties and wedding receptions than record company shindigs, but it was here in January 2011 that Ed Sheeran introduced his family to his new employers: Atlantic Records. Ed was there along with his mum and dad and brother Matthew. The paperwork had been signed at the Sheerans' family home. It had been revealed that Ed's music would be released on Asylum Records, which is now part of Atlantic. Asylum had been home to the likes of Joni Mitchell, Bob Dylan and the Eagles in the early 1970s – right up the Sheerans' street. After lying fallow for several years the label was revived in the early noughties, signing hip hop and urban acts, including Cee Lo Green and Sheeran's hero Wiley.

Asylum's managing director Ben Cook was at the party, along with the label's A&R manager Ed Howard and Sheeran's manager Stuart Camp. 'This is where it all started and this is my home,' Sheeran told the *East Anglian Daily Times* as family and record company bosses mingled and had their pictures taken supping pints. Even teetotal Ed was snapped with a pint in hand. 'It's nice for everyone to meet each other, have a pub meal and taste the beer. It was a long time coming so I feel happy. It's a new stage that's starting and I felt it was time to happen,' he said.

'We're so proud of Ed and very happy that he has realised what he set out to do,' Ed's mother Imogen told reporters as the group tucked into their pub lunches. Ed signed his contract – again – for the benefit of the local television news cameras. He told reporters he'd received a congratulatory call from Sir Elton John, who was part of the same management group. Sheeran said he'd acted very cool when talking to him on the phone: 'Oh, hey how's it going? But as soon as I was off the phone it was... wow. Surreal.'

Ed also revealed that there had been some disquiet among his more fervent supporters about him signing to a major label and losing his independent status. 'A lot of people were happy about it and a lot of people were saying please don't sell out,' he told reporters. 'The great thing about releasing all the EPs independently is that when you sign to a label, they say you can make the album you want to make, with the songs you want on it. So the fans have to be happy because there's no way I can sell out because I'm allowed to do exactly what I want to do. I'm in a really good situation.'

Ben Cook, managing director of Asylum, said: 'Ed is a supremely talented singer-songwriter – he's the archetypal artist for our times. He's managed to amass a fervent and meaningful fan base entirely from his own efforts and got his EP in the charts. We're delighted to have signed him.'

Cook had actually highlighted a significant point – in signing his deal, Sheeran held nearly all the cards: he had the songs, the means to record them and the talent. But most importantly, he had the fan base and Ed was able to deliver them directly to the record company. Getting a deal and an advance was one thing, but Ed already had the most valuable asset: fans who would follow him wherever he went. All the record company had to offer was infrastructure. 'A deal doesn't really mean anything,' he explained to Baltimore 106.5. 'It's all about the people who work at the company. If they're no good then fuck your deal, it doesn't really matter. You could get 500 grand for your deal and still flop. I got a very small amount for my deal, but at Atlantic I got some of the best press, some of the best TV pluggers... that's the reason it's worked, not the money side of it.'

Ed had decided to continue his association with Jake Gosling and the producer was pleased with Sheeran's decision to sign with Atlantic/Asylum. 'I had worked with Asylum before and knew Ed Howard and Ben Cook well from when I had produced the *See Clear Now* album for Wiley,' Gosling wrote on his blog. 'Ed needed to feel that they were the right home for his music and after several meetings and talks alongside his manager Stuart Camp the whole move felt right and so Ed put pen to paper.'

Never one to take his foot off the pedal, Ed revealed he had already started work on his debut, non-independent album: 'I've been in the studio all this week,' he said, 'and will be all next week and the one after. I hope the album will out in August or September. I've also got lots of TV and radio and promotion to do. It's mental – really cool, though.'

The first thing that Ed had to get used to was that he didn't have to do everything himself anymore. Years of self-reliance meant that he was in the habit of being in control. Now he had to loosen the reigns a bit. 'It's been a cool transition, although it was a bit weird to start with,' he told the I Love Music website. 'To start with I was still booking all my own interviews, doing my own press, uploading videos myself, leaking songs and stuff. I've just had to get around to the fact that there's a professional way of doing stuff and it doesn't all have to be out there, you know? It can be held back when it's like the big deal, so yeah; I've kind of adjusted in that sense. It's just wicked to have such a nice team around me. They're just all really, really lovely people that actually genuinely want you to succeed. They're not just doing it for the graphs and charts, they actually really like the music and they're at every single show without fail. They're just really nice people. They're cool to hang out with as well, you know – I go out to the cinema with my project manager, I live on my manager's sofa, I go out for dinner with my A&R all the time... it's just really nice. It isn't like a business, it's like a family.'

There would have been questions swirling around Sheeran and his team as the album began to come together. Which Ed Sheeran would the album represent? There were plenty to choose from. Full band or stripped back? Folkie or indie? Grime or loop? 'I started recording in January in a friend's garden shed in Suffolk,' Ed later told *Q* magazine. 'I wanted to keep that organic, lo-fi feel. I've got the rest of my life to make an album in a plush studio. This time around I wanted to stay true to the sound that got me this far. I went in with pretty much all the songs written, but a couple popped out while we were recording.'

It wasn't long before his friend's shed was left behind and Ed returned to the familiar surroundings of Jake Gosling's Sticky Studios, though the lo-fi feel remained. 'We wanted to keep the album organic and real, not to overproduce it – let it breathe,' Gosling explained to *The Guardian*. 'You can hear squeaky chairs, coughing and birds outside the studio. I remember the label going on and on about how they could hear the breaths and wanting me to take them out. I told them I liked the breaths – he's breathing, he's not a machine. It's all about songs, stories and real feelings – things people can relate to. For a period of time that got lost and it was all about being in a club, popping bottles of champagne. Kids are being spoon-fed premeditated stuff older people think they'll like, with hook after hook after hook. They think people can't handle deeper lyrics, that it's too dark, too depressing – but via the internet we proved them wrong.

Ed really knows what he wants as an artist, and I think that's so important. A lot of artists don't, they don't even know who they are. If you got that identity and know what you will and won't do – and if you work extremely hard – then you're setting yourself up for a good thing. But you still need labels.'

Ed: 'It's a very cool thing to be signed, but only because it's the right major [label],' he told the *East Anglian Daily Times*. 'It was the best time to sign a deal because I did it when I didn't need to do it. It meant the label didn't call the shots. It's a symbiotic relationship. It's no different to being an independent artist – the only thing is I don't have to sort things out. I don't have to ring up magazines anymore. I'm just sitting back, making music and doing gigs – and focussing on being professional.'

As the album began to take shape, it became clear that this was going to be very much an 'in-house' affair, with all of the songs coming from the Gosling/Sheeran partnership. Only one song came from outside Sticky Studios: 'Kiss Me'. Ed had gone to Los Angeles for an exploratory writing session with producer No ID, otherwise known as Dion Wilson. Wilson – No ID is Dion backwards – is best known for producing the likes of Jay-Z, Kanye West and Nas. 'Ed did quite a few tracks out there,' producer Gosling told music writer Tom Doyle. 'But that one really felt like it fitted with the rest of the album. It worked with the sound that I'd created. It tied in really nicely.'

Perhaps it worked out even more nicely with No ID than Gosling imagined. 'I had a few sessions with him (No ID),'

Sheeran later told the Urban Development website, 'and I think I'm gonna do the second album with him.'

Despite No ID's rap credentials, Sheeran warned fans not to expect the expected. 'It's like a proper, full-on, wedding dance love song,' is how Sheeran described 'Kiss Me' to Rap-UP TV. 'You kind of expect No ID to do hip hop, but we did a slow jam instead.'

The song that caused the most problems during the sessions wasn't a new song, but the oldest one: 'You Need Me, I Don't Need You', which Ed had been tinkering with since he was 15. More than 20 attempts were made to get the track the way that both Sheeran and Gosling wanted it. Initial attempts to recapture the live and looped feel of Ed's SB.TV version failed to harness the same magic – it was clear that the version Sheeran had put online was a one-off. 'The problem we had was that the first recording that was done was a live SB.TV thing and the energy and atmosphere of that track was what we wanted to capture,' Gosling explained. 'Of course, with the magic of music and the way it goes, you can't always capture that again. So we really struggled. We did so many different versions: full-on drummy things and really stripped-back stuff. Then we tried to do it how we recorded it originally, with the loop pedal. We even thought of actually using the original loop pedal track, but it was only recorded in stereo. But everyone loved the song and Ed really wanted it to be a single as well, so we eventually had enough of it. It was like, "We can't take this anymore, we've done 20 versions."'

Ed's record label suggested drafting in producer Charlie

Hugall – who'd worked with Florence + the Machine, Kaiser Chiefs and Eliza Doolittle – to work on the track, particularly the drum patterns. Hugall's remix became the final version, so a problem with a song about record industry suits telling artists what to do, was essentially settled by record industry suits telling the artist and the producer what to do. Gosling was philosophical about the situation: 'I don't think everyone knows the answers,' he said in an interview with *Sound on Sound*. 'Even if you've got a really good clear idea, at the same time, sometimes it can help to give the record company's ideas a go. If it doesn't work, it doesn't work. But with that song, I think we got to a place where we were all happy with it.'

Sheeran was still connected to the outside world while recording was taking place – he'd embraced Twitter with the same enthusiasm that he'd embraced other social media. In fact he had to take a break from tweeting while the album was being made, as his keenness for Twitter was getting in the way of work. 'I'm trying not to use Twitter too much actually,' he told the BBC. 'When I was off it for two weeks making the record, people thought I'd died.'

At Sticky Studios, many of the sessions would start with Gosling just talking to Sheeran, quizzing him about what was going on in his life: 'As a producer and songwriter, it's my job to be almost like a psychiatrist,' Gosling later said. '"Tell me your problems, Ed. What's going on with your life?"'

One thing that was going on in Ed's life would seep into the album – his relationship with his girlfriend. 'Every single one of the love songs I've written has been about her,' he told *The Star*, making it clear that it was Alice who kept his feet on the ground. 'It's nice to know I've got a girlfriend who gave a shit [about me] in the first place before the fame thing kicked off.'

As the songs came together, it was clear that Ed's girlfriend would be the common theme that bound the album together, essentially opening up their relationship for all to see. 'I think she'll be a bit embarrassed people all over the UK know our personal stories,' Ed later told Scotland's *Daily Record*. 'But she won't be bothered about an album being written about her. The reasons I like her so much is she's not fussed about that.'

Not one to let something like his 20th birthday get in the way of his first 'proper' album, Ed spent 17 February in the studio. As a thank you to fans he performed relaxed covers of songs online, choosing songs by Adele, Jessie J and Nizlopi as they took his fancy. As was finishing he noticed how late it was. 'Girlfriend's going to be pissed,' he said before signing off.

Ed's relationship with Alice wouldn't survive the release of his debut album. 'It ended because I've been on tour for six months and seen her twice,' he told the *Daily Record*. 'She's at university and it wasn't good.' Despite this, Ed seemed to cling on to the notion that all was not lost with the relationship: 'I'll probably end up marrying her I reckon, but for now it's not going to work out.'

The detail of what happened was to be found on a track given away to fans as a free download. The *One Take EP* –

'something old, something new, something blues' as Ed described it – featured a looped-up Sticky Studios version of 'You Need Me, I Don't Need You', his one-man-band take on traditional spiritual song 'Wayfaring Stranger' and an unfamiliar tune: 'Uni'. Here, Sheeran is the stoned sap, heartbroken because he's split up with his girlfriend who's been away at university. She's in the halls of residence, he's on a tour bus. But even when he's spilling his guts, Sheeran can't resist a bit of wordplay, as he details how you and I (u 'n' i) were pulled apart because of uni. Boom, boom...

Sheeran's quoted intention of 'marrying her some day' was not to be. Not long after the break-up – and with Ed's profile rising – he was photographed with a 'girl who was just a friend, which was quite a shit thing to happen'. The photo was published and Sheeran was deeply concerned that the picture would be spotted by Alice and taken the wrong way. 'It was quite a difficult break-up after four years,' he later told *The Guardian*. 'I've not really spoken to her since and the first thing she sees is me in the paper with someone else.'

For now, Sheeran vowed to stay single: 'I might explore the ideas of someone else but, at the moment, I'm focused on my career,' he told the *Daily Record*. 'My view is, if I couldn't make it work with someone I've gone out with for four years, then I shouldn't go out with anyone else just now.'

To celebrate the success of the free EP – 7,000 downloads on the first day – he decided to hold a free gig in London on 12 April. Ed announced the event online: 'OK then! The show is on Tuesday at the Barfly in Camden. Doors at 7pm, first come first served. It's a FREE gig and for those of you who can't get in, I'll do another one for you lot straight after I've played the first one. It's 14+ but people under 16 need to be with an adult. See you Tuesday!'

The twittersphere kicked in and by 2pm queues had already started to form outside the venue. Clearly something quite special was happening. Entertainment website Pyromag was on hand with an on-the-spot report: 'As Barfly was taken over by girls in denim shorts, baggy t-shirts and back-combed hair and skinny-jean-wearing guys, the excitement was on the verge of bubbling over. Sheeran proved so popular, his fans were tweeting at 2pm that they had already began queuing. And they just didn't stop, the queue was rumoured to be a thousand-plus. During the gig, he commented on how humble he felt when he was performing to 30 people a year ago and how it's unreal that he now had a crowd of this size to perform to. Pyromag estimates the crowds are going to grow and grow as his talent is undeniable and he is so likeable.'

The more Sheeran played, the more fans turned up at the Barfly. He played a second and then a third show. The change in Ed's fortunes was there for all to see. For someone who was playing to handfuls of people a matter of months earlier, this was a dramatic turnaround. 'It was a nice moment,' Ed later recalled of the Barfly performances in an interview with the *Daily Telegraph*. 'Really humbling. It makes a change from playing shows where only two people turn up but those shows are important too. You still have to play well. 'Cos they have to walk away from it thinking, That was all right, I'd like to go and see him again.'

The venue was preparing to close but there were still Sheeran fans waiting to see him play. In the end, Sheeran had to take to the street outside the venue to play unplugged to satisfy demand: 'I didn't expect that many kids to turn up,' Sheeran later told *IP1*.'So I played three 45-minute shows indoors and then another show outside after the place closed.'

Surrounded by camera phones and with manager Stuart Camp by his side, the sight of Sheeran playing live outside the venue is an extraordinary one. The fans – the *faithful* – are so carried away by the moment their singing keeps putting him off. They are inches away from Sheeran as he tries and tries to get 'You Need Me' underway. 'That always fucks me up!' he cries as the crowd's singing puts him off the beat. He tries again – only to fail once more. The fans' affection towards Sheeran is overwhelming – it's fascinating and slightly scary at the same time. As he sings the lines of the song that mention being filmed, he puts his face into a young woman's camera phone. She screams. *Really* screams. 'I haven't got used to the screams yet,' he later told the *Daily Telegraph*. 'I'm not exactly boy band material, am I?'

The Barfly gig would prove to be a key indicator of how Sheeran's star was rising. The next would be how quickly he was selling out dates for his upcoming tour. Another would come at the end of April – and it was a dream come true: he was asked to appear on *Later With Jools Holland*. The former Squeeze keyboard player and presenter of *The Tube* had carved himself a muso niche for discerning music fans with his BBC2 programme. Its mix of classic artists, new acts and left-of-centre world music had established Holland as a tastemaker – for a relatively unknown artist like Sheeran to appear on the programme often meant that fame was just around the corner. 'I was really, really nervous,' he later confessed to the Urban Development website. 'It was quite a weird thing because it all happened at the last minute, it was all live and it's a big show to do. I was shitting myself, not literally but, yeah.'

With his parents in the audience, Ed performed a slightly pacier, in-your-face version of 'The A Team'. He also provided a looped-up voice and beatbox version of the spiritual standard 'Wayfaring Stranger' for *Later*'s sister programme *Later Live*. For Sheeran, it meant he had arrived. 'When I did that, from an industry point of view, it set the seal,' he told the BBC. 'I felt like, this is really happening, it's really serious – it's not just a fluke on iTunes.'

As is often the case with *Later*, there were stars dotted around the studio audience and this edition was no different. Ed: 'It was great for my dad to sit on a table next to Ringo Starr in the audience.' For the Sheerans, sitting next to Starr must surely have cast their minds back to those long car journeys from West Yorkshire to London, listening to The Beatles.

On 12 June 'The A Team' was finally released as Ed's first single. It had been an EP track on *Loose Change* in the past, and the video had already been viewed a million times on YouTube, so for many fans it must have felt like an old favourite rather than a debut single, though it was backed up by a full package of remixes. Ed was sent out onto the promotional trail to publicise the single, doing 'six or seven interviews a day' up and down the country. With the PR machine of Atlantic/Asylum behind it, the fact that it had been playlisted by Radio 1 and a ready-made fan base eager to show their support, the single sold 57,607 copies in its first week and got to Number 3 in the singles chart, just behind Calvin Harris and Ed's friend Example. 'It's cool to have a song in the Top 10 that isn't a dance tune and I really appreciate that people took a risk on the song,' he told BBC Suffolk. 'Having a song about a heroin-addicted prostitute get mainstream success is a really cool thing I think. I got a text from my manager with the figures of what we'd sold and what everyone else had sold.'

It's believed that Sheeran celebrated the news of his debut single's success with a milkshake on Falmouth beach. But was there just a whiff of disappointment that it hadn't gone to UK Number 1? 'It had been Number 3 since Wednesday, so I was still incredibly happy but not as surprised as I was on Tuesday when I found out the midweek,' he said. 'It's a really respectful number to go in with a debut single.'

Perhaps more importantly, the single opened him up to an international audience, with the song eventually going Top 10 in Australia, New Zealand and Japan. Reviewers were kind overall with many of the more mainstream media outlets introducing Sheeran to their readers for the first time. Digital Spy clearly admired Ed's work and his work ethic: 'In an age where a star is born in a matter of weeks we were beginning to think that the traditional path to success of hard graft and persistence had been wiped out. Thankfully, Ed Sheeran – after three years, 600 live shows and five self-released EPs – proves there's life in the old gal yet with his first mainstream release, "The A Team". Yes, the man-and-his-guitar concept is about as cliché as they come, but it's his intelligent lyrics and softer-than-cream-cheese vocals that set him apart from the pack. The true story of a homeless drug addict who will "go mad for a couple grams" and whose face is "crumbling like pastries", Sheeran's frank honesty and lump-in-the-throat-like emotion are weighted by a folky melody and off-kilter acoustics. It might have taken him a while to get here, but as the saying goes, slow and steady.'

Online entertainment magazine Pyromag said: '"The A Team" tells the story of a young, homeless drug addict and at just 20 years old, Ed tells it with a maturity beyond his years. The lyrics are very powerful and deep and the vocals effortless, making a song with a dark, depressing undertone sound beautiful. With a complete remix package, legendary producers Shy FX, True Tiger and Koan Sound bring their unique twist to the original version.'

'Lacking distinct emotion, he sings with a hauntingly voyeuristic nature that forces the listener to question the validity of the song's lyrics,' said the Altsounds website. 'Is it actually a true story? Is Sheeran writing about someone he knows? Is he describing an experience he would rather forget? Despite all of its simplicity, there is a degree of depth that Sheeran explores throughout the song's entirety that cannot be messed with.'

Producer Jake Gosling was happy with what he and Sheeran had achieved. 'I think a lot more people are wanting deeper music and lyrics and stories, rather than another pop track singing about the club,' he said. 'In terms of album artists, people are wanting real songs, especially the younger generation. But, yeah, it's been a lot of hard work and sweat and tears and all the rest of it that goes into it. And Ed sleeping on my sofa. He loves his sofas. I'm gonna buy him a sofa. Actually, I might just give him my sofa. Which he's wrecked by the way. It doesn't fold up properly any more.'

Mindful that some of the material on the album would be familiar to some, Ed wanted to leave an indicator of where he was heading next. He did it in the shape of the last track 'Give Me Love'. 'That's an important song for me,' he told Q magazine. 'It's got a more fleshed out sound, which is where I'm headed in the future.'

It was decided that the album's title would be just a symbol: +.

It conjured thoughts of positivity – a very Ed Sheeran thing to do – but it also fulfilled a very practical, business-savvy purpose too, another Sheeran trademark: it protected his living and would make it tricky to illegally download the album. 'You can't Google it so it's quite hard to find it on torrenting sites,' he explained to journalist Sam Parker. 'I have to make a living and musicians don't make that much money these days. People think because you're on the TV you're a millionaire, but we still have to make money. I've never illegally downloaded anything, I've always bought CDs.'

NINE

I APOLOGISE
FOR MY FANS

Ed's summer prior to the release of + was dominated by festival performances. He was voted Best Breakthrough Act 2011 for his performances at – among others – Bestival, Reading, Jersey Live and multiple stints at a rather swampy Glastonbury at the UK Festival Awards.

Despite his growing profile, his increasing position as a live draw and the fact that he had a major record deal, Ed said that things for him had stayed largely as they were. 'Life has changed a lot but it's kind of gradually changed over time so I haven't noticed it that much,' he told the Urban Development website. 'I'm still in the same position, I still live on my manager's sofa, still with a rucksack and a guitar playing gigs, so it hasn't changed in terms of how I am but more people are listening to my music, and I'm playing at bigger shows.'

As a trailer for the album, 'You Need Me, I Don't Need You' – the song that Ed had attempted to capture so many times during the album sessions – was released as a single in August. Co-producer Charlie Hugall's version with its clattering beats and whoops gave the track a fresh lick of paint, but the main addition to the song was the video that accompanied it. Emil Nava – best known at that stage for Jessie J's 'Do It Like a Dude' and 'Price Tag' videos – created a stark monochrome studio landscape for the song, which details Sheeran's story so far. It would be the first of many collaborations between the two. 'Emil will always do my videos as long as he wants to,' Ed later told SB.TV. 'He's phenomenal and he has great ideas. Ever since we sat down and worked out the "You Need Me" video I knew I wanted him to do all my videos.'

Nava believes it's Sheeran's desire not to appear in the videos that makes them so good. 'Ed prefers to not be in the video so much, so that gives me the opportunity to push the idea more, so the sign language one was a dream to make.'

Though there are hip hop dancers and flashes of Sheeran himself, the video is totally dominated by teenage actor Matthew Morgan, performing the lyrics in British Sign Language (BSL). 'Matt is a wicked guy,' Sheeran told BBC News. 'He's an actor and we wanted to make a music video for that song that kind of hadn't been done before – which everyone says about music videos – but we found a concept that hadn't been done which was sign language to highlight the lyrical aspect to it. We auditioned a few people and Matt popped up. He's got a really striking face and he kind of connects with the camera. Both his parents are deaf but he's not so he knows how to do BSL fluently. He's just amazing.'

Sign language purists will point out that the video isn't 'full' BSL, as Morgan's face hardly moves a muscle during the song. Facial expression is a vital part of sign language – watch the signers in the bottom corner of your TV screen next time they pop up late at night – but the video seemed to delight the deaf community, with the School of Sign Language predicting that the song could kick off a trend for using BSL in music videos.

Given that the song had already been released as an EP track and was available in a variety of styles online, it's fair to say that the video must have played a vital role in getting the single to Number 4 in the charts, along with the guest appearances from Wretch 32 and Devlin on the accompanying remixes.

When + was released on 12 September, Sheeran fans might have been forgiven for thinking that his first album for a major label was less of a debut and more of a 'Best Of'. Of the 13 tracks (including a hidden track) five had already been released in one form or other before the album came out. The album opens with 'The A Team' – a song that dates back to 2010's *Loose Change* EP, as well as the Mikill Pane version on *No.5 Collaborations*.

The first fresh track comes next: 'Drunk'. It appears to detail the two things Ed misses the most: drinking and his former girlfriend Alice. 'She's pretty much what the album is about,' he told *Q* magazine when asked if he'd used his feelings about the break-up to inspire his writing. 'It's cool. I wrote some good songs.' The backing on the track is a minimal mix of echoing guitar, tight and high drums and a reasonable portion of Sheeran wordplay as he puns his way through lyrics on lipsticks and Coldplay. Two tracks in and the mood for the album is set: the sound and the production are cut back to the bone. 'I think the power really comes from the words and the sonics that are there,' producer Jake Gosling explained to *Sound on Sound*. 'I wanted to make sure that they were right, rather than filling up and overcomplicating the tracks. We wanted it to be quite stripped back and to give it a lot of space. I think a lot of music tends to be overfilled these days. People shove everything in it. What we were aiming to do was let the songs breathe.'

'U.N.I.' is next. Compared to the *One Take* version it's lush stuff, a fuller take on Sheeran's tale of lovers separated by the conflicting schedules of education and touring. It's quiet and regretful in its tone and deserves its place on the track listing. 'Grade 8' is commercial to the point of being a touch corporate. Lyrically it's a little distant compared to Sheeran's usual work – it's normally fairly easy to work out what he's is getting at; on 'Grade 8' it's more about tone than clarity and the song could just as easily be sung by Rihanna as it could by Ed.

'Wake Me Up' – last heard on *Live at the Bedford* – strips away what little instrumentation was on offer and takes it down to just Sheeran plus piano chords plus silence. Ed played the piano himself on the track. Sheeran's phrasing, particularly towards the end of the track, is pure Luke Concannon. It's shamelessly soppy stuff, particularly when put against the next song, 'Small Bump'. It's a beautifully restrained tale of a young dad and a premature baby – just as the song is getting settled into the territory occupied by Athlete's 'Wires', Sheeran pulls the rug from under us and snatches the baby away.

'This' almost feels like a post-Alice song as he charts the start of a new relationship. Again, things are kept sparse: it's Ed, his guitar and the lurking presence of Damien Rice. 'The City' is the song that dates back to Sheeran's first writing session with Jake Gosling when Ed was just 16. There are some additional bleeps and a touch of distorted guitar, but the arrangement largely sticks to the human beatbox and looping style previously established. There was concern among Sheeran's fans that he would jettison the looping altogether for the album, but as the loop pedal was a key part of the Sheeran live experience, it became an essential part of the album's process. 'Because that was his main performance thing, we'd often write in a loop way,' Gosling later explained. 'We'd loop up a beat and a guitar part and build it from there, working through dropping the track out or cutting it back in, like you would use a loop pedal.'

Next up is 'Lego House', co-written with Jake Gosling and Chris Leonard, former guitarist with Son of Dork, the band formed by James Bourne after Busted split up. 'I wrote this song back in 2009,' Sheeran later told *The*

Guardian. 'It was basically a song about a realisation period. The way I wrote it with Jake originally was in a dub step tempo with really minimal drums. Instead of guitar we just used strings and I wrote the top line over that. The lyrics were already written in my phone. I just rhymed in couplets and I just tried to be really imaginative – I didn't want to write a really basic love song, I wanted to use stuff like Lego and painting by numbers. It took about a day to write.'

The song was an excuse to reference the toy that had not only been his favourite as a child, but was still a favourite now. The list of requirements for Ed when he played a gig now had a new addition: 'One small box of Lego'. 'It sounds really weird, but it's how I relax,' he explained to *Q* magazine. 'Cos when you make Lego, you're so engrossed with the instructions and finding the little bits and putting it all together, you don't think about anything else. And you're doing it for six or seven hours, so you just switch off and make it. When you're done, you just go back to your normal life. I've loved Lego since I was born.'

The outsourced version of 'You Need Me, I Don't Need You' comes next before things are taken right down to the two-in-the-morning sound of 'Kiss Me'. A mix of drum samples and bluesy guitar, the writing credits for the song include Julie Frost, a songwriter who's had a hand in tracks by everyone from Beyonce to Madonna. Justin Franks – aka DJ Frank E – also gets a credit; he's worked with Madonna as well as Justin Bieber and Kanye West.

Despite all the stellar names it's the most traditional, almost backward-looking track on offer, as if it's been designed for the US market.

The final track is 'Give Me Love,' the song that Sheeran said was the indicator of where he was heading next. If that's the case then Damien Rice can take it easy for the next few years because Ed clearly has that territory well and truly covered. It's Sheeran at his most Rice-like and confessional before the track builds into a handclaps-and-screaming finale.

But there's one more song to come, a hidden track, 'The Parting Glass'. A rather mournful traditional drinking song, it's been attempted by many artists including Sinéad O'Connor and The Pogues. Even Pierce Brosnan has had a swing at it in the film *Evelyn*. Sheeran and Gosling tried the song as a simple piano and vocal take before throwing it out and coming up with a haunting arrangement that involved multiple sampling of Ed humming the background chorus. Apart from the many and varied takes of 'You Need Me', the song was the only other track on the album that caused producer Jake Gosling sleepless nights. 'The reason why is because it's all vocally done,' he explained to journalist Tom Doyle. 'The backing vocals were all played on a keyboard and each note was sung four times, so you can imagine how long that took. We'd solo one note and Ed would sing that note four times, down and down the keyboard to the bass, as low as he could go basically. It hadn't sounded right with piano and vocal, so it was like, Well, let's trying humming it.'

The effort was worth it – it's a lovely attempt at an old favourite and a nice nod to Sheeran's folky and Irish roots. The reason it was listed as a hidden track rather than track number 13? 'Thirteen tracks is unlucky!' he told *Hot Press*. 'I was not gonna put out an album with 13 tracks. I'm not superstitious, but if the album flopped, I'd be like, that's why!'

The album was done and copies were sent to reviewers. Sheeran seemed to almost prepare himself for the worst in terms of the critical reaction he would get. 'Any review of this album is irrelevant,' he posted online to his fans. 'As long as you like it, that really is the only review I'll be reading or caring about.'

As the first tracks were being listened to, Sheeran revealed that he was already working on the follow-up. 'I'm already piecing together songs for the next LP,' he told *Q* magazine. 'Your second album is much more important than your first. Sometimes acts don't take enough time to make a second record and it falls under the radar. It needs to be like Coldplay, a phenomenal debut followed by an even more phenomenal second record. A first album is a first step, but a second needs to cement you in position. You have to smash it, basically.'

The reviews that accompanied the release of + were the very definition of the word 'mixed'. Initially, Ed seemed to take this rather personally: 'I think I got one good review,' he later claimed in an interview with *The Guardian*, 'in the *Halifax Courier* or something.'

He was clearly being oversensitive because there *were*

glowing notices. *Q* magazine, probably Britain's most respected music monthly, stated their view clearly at the head of their review: 'Fresh-faced wunderkind aces his debut'. 'If music were just about hard work, Ed Sheeran would have it made,' said *Q* reviewer Chris Cottingham, referring to Sheeran's famed work ethic. '+ is remarkable, fully formed and, for the most part, executed with maturity and skill. All that hard graft, it seems, has paid off in full.'

Andy Gill for *The Independent* also seemed to be on board: 'Right now, whoever used to be Ed Sheeran's manager is probably feeling like Decca's Dick Rowe must have in the years following his rejection of The Beatles. But in the ex-manager's case, things have been made just that bit more humiliating by Sheeran's decision to follow up his huge hit single "The A Team" with the brutal kiss-off "You Need Me, I Don't Need You" ... He's right to trust his own instincts ... Sheeran might have wound up with a respectable, if predictable, career as a mainstream folkie singer-songwriter rocking the outer reaches of Radio 2... Instead, he's a bona fide hitmaker.'

The *Daily Express*'s view was a little cooler: 'This is one of those rags-to-slightly-better-rags stories of a 16-year-old country lad who turns up in London with nothing but a guitar and a dream and a couple of years later is being called a songwriting phenomenon by music bible *Q*. It's easy to laugh but there is a lot to like about 20-year-old Ed Sheeran's debut. The songs range from fairly trad folk to speedily sung tracks that owe quite a bit to hip hop. While it remains to be seen if he has the charisma to properly make it, on the evidence of this it's looking good.'

But *The Observer* looked so far down on the album – and its likely audience – that it's surprising they could see the cover: 'Lad-next-door troubadour Ed Sheeran is indebted to artists such as Jamie T and Damien Rice, as evidenced by a debut that hops between bullish mockney rap and quavering sentimentality, but there's also a Bieber-ish quality to his appeal. There are the 20-year-old's almost 300,000 Twitter followers for one thing but, more dubiously, he and Biebz share a tendency to address their songs to vulnerable teenage girls. Half-rapped banalities about watching *Shrek* 12 times and being "crap at computer games" will certainly win hearts, but perhaps only those of a certain age.'

The Bieber reference would particularly rankle with Sheeran: 'A lot of people seem to think I'm a kind of British Justin Bieber and it's only girls that are into me,' he complained to *The Guardian*. 'But it's really a 50/50 thing.'

The *NME* – the last man standing of British rock music weeklies – was also far from complimentary. Giving the album 4/10, the paper's Emily Mackay said: 'Ed Sheeran has been ticking integrity-boxes so fast you can practically hear his hands still whirring in the background of his debut album. He's got the touches of "urban" styling with flimsy hip hop rhythms and Plan B-lite veering between half-arsed rapping and boy band emoting. He's got the "issues" songs (the Dido-ish, maudlin "Drunk", the omnipresent saccharine horror of the drugs/homelessness/prostitution triple-whammy of "The A Team"). He's got the unimpeachable DIY back story. The funniest thing is how dated and tame it all sounds coming from someone with such obvious drive to succeed. There's little here that's moves on from the kind of trip-hop balladeers that abounded in the late '90s or indeed the singer-songwriters that Sheeran admires such as Damien Rice (whose presence is felt on 'The Parting Glass', the Celtic-tinged folky lament that closes the album) or James Morrison.'

Despite Sheeran's protestations that he didn't care about reviews, that one must surely have left a mark. It was a review by *The Guardian*'s Alex Petridis, however, that generated the quickest and most dramatic response. 'From the title down, his current hit "You Need Me, I Don't Need You" presents 20-year-old singer songwriter Ed Sheeran as a very cocksure customer indeed ... But his cottage-industry past and chumminess with Wiley notwithstanding, Sheeran is an utterly mainstream artist: "The A Team", for example, is essentially Phil Collins's "Another Day in Paradise" for the Moshi Monsters generation... At its worst, + is a pretty winsome business.'

Petridis later claimed that almost immediately after the review was published, he was inundated by online messages from hardcore Sheeran fans – the so called Sheeranators – defending their idol's honour. 'A few hours after my three-star review of his album was published, they went totally banzai on Twitter, sending me messages filled with abuse of various stripes and degrees of literacy,' Petridis later wrote. 'One of them told me I was a terrible writter (sic). Others took a remarkably profane approach.'

It probably didn't help Petridis that he'd he wrongly attributed the rap on the extended online versions of 'You Need Me' – a nod to the Laid Blak track 'Red' – to Sheeran himself, accusing the 21-year-old of styling himself as a gangsta, describing it as 'a freestyle rap about smoking dope, alas delivered in a mock-Jamaican accent – that even the song's most ardent fan might perhaps consider a little too much of a good thing: "Where I come from, burning weed is a habit ... something I've inherited like a ghetto man should," offers Sheeran, who comes from Framlingham in Suffolk, a market town voted the No 1 place to live in Britain by *Country Life* magazine.'

Sheeran had to step in and call for calm, but perhaps there was also a sense he was secretly thrilled at his fans' devotion. 'They're militant, aren't they? Crazy. I love them,' he told journalist Sam Parker. 'I think the reason is that they've grown with me from a point and lived my success with me. I am good to them I think. They're just normal, lovely people.' Several months down the line, *The Guardian* mischievously sent Petridis out to interview Sheeran face to face. 'I apologise for my fans,' Ed told the journalist. 'They're ... they're definitely in my corner.'

At first Sheeran seemed genuinely rattled by some of the less than glowing reviews like the one served up by

Petridis, despite his protestations to the contrary. 'Remember, reviewers don't buy albums, they just listen to it once and do a five-minute review of it. So I don't really care about what Alexis Petridis has to say. His job is to review an album, and if he doesn't like it he'll give it a bad review. I'm fine with that. What I would care about is if a fan bought my album for £10.99 and said, "You know what Ed? This isn't up to scratch." Fuck it. As long as I do what I want and I'm happy with it, it will be fine. I think the worst thing is when people call other people sell-outs. If I had got that bad review from Alexis Petridis in *The Guardian* and thought, Oh fuck he's right ... that would be selling out. But I am 100% happy with everything I did on the album. I don't think I'll ever lose that. I come from a scene where we like to be credible and do what we want.'

Reviewers may not buy albums, but Sheeran fans did. The album sold more than 100,000 copies in its first week and went to Number 1. Ed posted the news online on his Twitter account: '+ is officially the #1 album in the uk!! We sold 102,350 copies this week! Thank you all so much, can't express how happy I am xxxx.'

The occasion had to be marked. Literally. A decision was made for as many people as possible involved in the album to get a + tattoo. Amy Wadge even travelled over from Wales to get hers done. Sheeran had been back to see her in Trefforest since their first writing session – she noticed a bit of a difference from the first time they'd met when he was an anonymous 17-year-old: 'I picked him up at the train station,' she told *Wales Online* about Ed's return, 'and he just got mobbed.'

Sheeran's tattoo was on his left wrist, joining the paw print he already had further up his arm. The event was captured on video by keen cinematographer Jamal Edwards of SB.TV, with a slightly queasy-looking Sheeran showing the tattoo to the camera. Ed took to Twitter to tell his fans: 'Just got my + tattoo, stings abit [sic].'

The inking was actually quite mild compared to Sheeran's original plan. 'The MD [of his record company] said he'd get a + tattooed on his forehead if we did a million records in a week,' he claimed in an interview with OTUmusic. 'So I'm going to speak to the head of the whole company and see if we can sell the record for 1p for the first week. Then I'll take out a big mortgage advance thing from the bank, then I'll buy a million copies and he'll have to get it tattooed on his forehead.'

Sheeran was refreshingly unembarrassed about admitting the scale of his ambitions, often referring to other acts as 'competition'. Many singers take the 'I'm just playing the music I like, if anyone else likes it that's a bonus' approach. Not Ed: he was determined it was possible to convince people to buy a million copies. That was the scale of the task and Ed felt he was up to it: 'I'm not afraid of hard work,' he told the Press Association. 'I'm not ashamed to say I'm hugely ambitious, and I dream of Coldplay-sized fame. Their music has grown to fill the venues they're playing – from rooms to arenas to stadiums, and that's where I want to be one day. I know

it's all about the songs, though, and the amount of work
you're prepared to put in. And I'm fully prepared to put
the effort in.'

TEN

#HOWSHITISEDSHEERAN

It was decided that 'Lego House' was to be the next single lifted from the album – and that meant it was time to get Emil Nava on the case with a new video. He outdid himself this time and produced one of the most peculiar mainstream music videos for a long time. But there was a problem. For the idea he and Sheeran came up with, they needed a young man with ginger hair who could act and who looked a lot like Ed Sheeran. 'Lots of people say I look like Ron Weasely,' Ed explained to *Fuse*. 'So I thought I'd poke fun at that and get Rupert Grint to play me in the video. So I reached out to Tom Feltham who plays Draco Malfoy in the films and he got in touch with Rupert... and Rupert said yes.'

Grint had a simpler explanation: 'It came about because

we're both... ginger,' he told MSN. 'When you see the video it'll all make sense. It was a lot of fun – very different – but a good laugh.'

The video was filmed at the ExCel conference centre in London's Docklands and at a real-life gig at the Hatfield Forum venue in Hertfordshire. The crew took the crowd by surprise by pulling Grint onstage, dressed in Sheeran-style hoodie and t-shirt. Grint even wore Ed's mother's trademark jewellery in the shoot. 'He was really fun to work with, really professional, really chilled. It was freaky to see him in the same clothes as me, he really does look like me. And I look like him.'

Sheeran prepared his fans for what they were about to witness: 'Just seen the "Lego House" video,' he tweeted on 20 October. 'Oh. My. Word.'

In the video, Grint is Ed Sheeran: tousled-haired troubadour and sensitive soul, lip-synching his way through the song. It seems like a fairly tame joke until the truth is revealed – Grint is in fact a stalker, breaking into Sheeran's tour bus, being manhandled off stage at Ed's gig and eating Sheeran's old chewing gum that he's kept in a scrapbook. The *Harry Potter* star – often criticised for his lack of acting chops – is terrific in the video, managing to be funny, charming and menacing all within the space of four minutes. A million people watched it in the first 48 hours it was online.

Sheeran took a very minor role in proceedings, briefly coming face to face with Grint as he exits a lift as the stalker is escorted from the building. 'I'm not really a music video kind of guy,' Ed explained to SB.TV. 'I make music because I love music. I didn't start writing songs and doing gigs so I could start making music videos. The reason I didn't appear in all the first videos is that I saw videos as ways to enhance the song, not to push me out as a product or as a face.'

The video was put out online to create a buzz for the single when it was released in November. Perhaps the video helped – 'Lego House' went to Number 5 in the UK charts – but Ed claimed he always knew the song was a hit. 'I didn't really expect it to take off with "The A Team", because of what it's about, but "Lego House", I kind of knew it would end up where it ended up if it got the right radio play,' he told *The Guardian*.

Meanwhile, one of Sheeran's favourite songs by his favourite singer was getting a fresh airing at around the same time. 'Cannonball' by Damien Rice – the song that had so enraptured Sheeran as an 11-year-old when he saw it on late-night TV – was the choice of song for the winner of 2011's *X Factor* show to release as a single. Sheeran had already popped up in a sense during that year's competition – the show's resident bad boy Frankie Cocozza had taken a swing at 'The A Team' earlier on in the series. He'd also made his Australian TV debut performing 'The A Team' on the Oz version of *The X Factor*.

Girl band Little Mix were the UK winners that year and clued-up interviewers were keen to get Sheeran's views on their take on 'Cannonball'. Though it started simply enough, the *X Factor* version had all the whistles and bells added, including that uplifting key change towards the end of the song so beloved of the competition's organisers. The press wanted to know what Ed thought: after all, a 'Sheeran versus *X Factor*' feud would make good copy. Sensing a potential trap was being laid for him, Ed chose his words carefully. 'They're lovely girls – I've met them, they're really nice,' he said of Little Mix to MSN. 'I don't necessarily think it was their choice [of song]. If there's one thing that song didn't need it was a key change and a choir. That's all I'm saying.'

The public seemed to agree with Ed. Although it went to Number 1, 'Cannonball' only sold 210,000 copies in its first week – less than half the amount shifted by Matt Cardle in 2011, when his Biffy Clyro cover 'When You Collide' sold 429,000 copies during its first week of release. One benefit of the song's exposure was that after all these years it was finally a fully fledged hit for Damien Rice. His original version went to Number 9, introducing it to a new generation of fans, something that must surely have pleased his most ardent supporter, Ed Sheeran.

The run up to Christmas also saw Ed involved in another single release, but one that didn't fare as well as 'Lego House'. Alongside the likes of Tulisa, Wretch 32, Rizzle Kicks and Labrinth, Sheeran was co-opted into performing on the 2011 Children in Need single. The track – under the banner of The Collective – was based on the Massive Attack song 'Teardrop'. The man behind the project was Take That's Gary Barlow but even before the single was released, Barlow seemed to hint that he was slightly out of his depth. 'It's been a bloody nightmare to organise,' he told *The Sun*.

'These guys are not easy, but we got them to the studio. It's the cream of UK talent. This is an area I don't exist in, so it's been an education. I played my part putting it together but I'm not on the song, I'm not cool enough. I didn't even produce it, that was down to Labrinth. They are the new generation coming through and they know what they are doing. Having me on it wouldn't have been right.'

Ed's voice is the first that you hear on the song, but unfortunately he's sort of talk/rapping, not singing, and his disinterested tone seems to set the song off on a bad foot. The whole enterprise has a rather preachy, hectoring tone – like of one of those school charity songs written by a well-meaning music teacher. Even dedicated Sheeran fans seemed to dislike the track and many made their feelings known on Ed's Facebook page: 'Sorry Ed, massive fan of you but hate this song' ... 'Bad song, sorry pal' ... 'I'll donate money for the great cause but I won't be buying the single' ... 'That is a massacre of a good song.'

The single was released on 13 November and staggered its way to Number 24 in the charts. It wasn't helped by some decidedly ropey live performances by The Collective, including one on Children in Need night where Tulisa's microphone wasn't switched on. It was the lowest chart performance for a Children in Need single for 16 years, when *EastEnders* stars Sid Owen and Patsy Palmer's single 'You Better Believe It' only managed to crawl to Number 60 in 1995.

It clearly did Sheeran no harm; music industry awards started to come his way. Soon there would be a growing pile at his door. In September he won Best Breakthrough Artist at the Digital Music Awards – Ed also performed at the ceremony, held at the Roundhouse in Camden. In October he won Best Single for 'The A Team' at the Radio 1 Teen Awards as well as Best Breakthrough Artist at the prestigious Q Awards. Tinie Tempah won Best Male at the ceremony. Tempah was clearly an Ed fan: he'd later describe Sheeran on Twitter as 'the coolest ever ginger'. Ed seemed to have his eye on the Best Male prize for the future: 'This is the award I wanted to win, because I don't think I'm at the stage yet where I can win Best Male, because someone like Tinie's been around for a bit and achieved much more. So to win Best Breakthrough is a nice stepping stone.'

That stepping stone didn't take long to reach. In January 2012 – as + returned to the top of the charts and was confirmed as going triple platinum – Ed was told he'd been nominated for four BRIT awards: Best Male, Breakthrough Act, Best Single for 'The A Team' and best album for +. For once, the level of recognition seemed to catch the usually calm and confident Sheeran off guard: 'I'm ecstatic, very over the moon,' he said when the nominations were announced. 'I'm just a bit surprised if I'm honest,' he told the BBC. The announcement ceremony for the nominations was made at the Savoy Hotel in London on a key anniversary date for Sheeran: 'It's quite weird actually – a year ago today I signed my record contract. Now I'm here. It's a bit mad.'

For a young man not known for his concern for sartorial arrangements, he did have one worry about the BRITS:

what to wear. 'The only problem is I usually wear baggy jeans and hoodies,' he told *The Sun*. 'Suits don't really do anything for me so I'm trying to get an odd suit made – still smart but with something different about it. I don't know if I can get a suit with a hood. I'll get one with quite a lot of orange in it to match my hair. It's mad to be performing on the night along with people like Coldplay and Adele. To be in a category with them is fantastic, but to be on the same stage is something I'm going to remember for a very long time.'

Ed Sheeran had very much arrived. If further proof was needed, it came with the news that 'Ed Sheeran' was the fourth most searched-for name on Google in the UK in 2011. Perhaps one of the reasons his name figured so highly was because of the number of searches carried out by one person in particular: Ed Sheeran. 'I actually Google myself every day because I often get bad things being said about me and I need to keep on that,' he confessed to Rap-Up TV. 'I think you need to know your enemies. If you have people telling you how amazing you are every day, you need people telling you that you're shit as well – just to keep you balanced.'

The New Year was looking good. Before Christmas Ed had announced he was setting up Paw Print Records to release all of his 'five-point plan' EPs under one umbrella. Describing them as the 'five EPs that got me where I am today', he tweeted: 'I'm excited to get them back out there, and even more excited that I own them and get to release them on my own label. Sickness :)'

His trophy cabinet had also been added to with an iTunes New Artist of the Year award. It's often the case that when an artist gets a rush of success and acclaim in the way Ed Sheeran had, it's followed by an equally swift backlash. Ed seemed prepared, even resigned to it: 'I just knew that I would end up in a position where the success would kind of take hold,' he told *The Guardian*. 'So people would either think you were intensely cool for your success or people would think you were shit for your success.'

There had been rumbles towards the end of 2011. In a piece in *The Guardian,* writer Peter Robinson labelled Sheeran and Adele as 'beige pop'. This was the age of The New Boring, he said, and Ed Sheeran was the chief culprit: 'The New Boring has found its posterboy in acoustic guitar-bothering singer-songwriter Ed Sheeran,' Robinson wrote in a funny and bitchy piece. 'Sheeran's music is like a combination of every friend-of-a-friend's band whose pub gig you have ever witnessed, and while most of us learn, during our twenties, how to sidestep these social disasters it is less easy to avoid when wedged quite so far up Radio 1's A-list. And it is no wonder the nation's favourite was quite so keen to embrace Sheeran: he combines the station's twin obsessions of authenticity (acoustic guitars!) with cool (he sometimes sort of half-raps and collaborates with urban people!). The music is... well, a David Guetta club jam it most certainly is not, and his album + is a 12-bore shitgun (13 if you include the bonus track).'

Asked by the same newspaper to respond to claims that he'd produced a '12-bore shitgun', Sheeran turned the accusation on its head: 'If Adele's seen as boring, then I'm happy to be boring as well,' he said.

But it was the *NME* that really threw in the fizzing bomb – and it truly backfired. There was a time when the *New Musical Express* (first published in 1952) ruled the roost among the 'inkies', the weekly rock music press that were the arbiters of taste in the pre-internet British music scene. No musical ground was too high for the paper to pontificate from, particularly in its late 1970s and early 1980s heyday. The paper's journalists liked to build 'em up, but they liked it even better when they were able to cut 'em down. But those days were long gone, as were the *NME*'s rivals: *Melody Maker, Sounds* and *Record Mirror*. The *NME* was the only weekly paper left and was by now a shadow of its former self. Occasionally, though, it still liked to rattle some cages – or at least, to be seen to. That's what seems to have happened as the paper approached its 60th birthday.

In January 2012 Luke Lewis, the editor of NME.com, had encouraged his Twitter followers, via *NME*'s account, to tweet their dislike of Sheeran's music. 'Objectively speaking,' Lewis asked the twittersphere, 'how shit is Ed Sheeran? I'll include your best responses in a blog post on Monday.'

Lewis believed this would encourage a 'funny and light hearted bit of banter'. He even took the trouble to create a special hashtag for the straw poll: *#howshitisedsheeran*. It quickly became apparent that Lewis' hashtag was not just generating banter, it was acting as a magnet for all manner of internet bile aimed at Sheeran; in Ed's words it 'became a vehicle for all sorts of crude and unfunny personal jibes.'

The fact that the focal point of this was the editor of NME.com and the *NME*'s Twitter account, gave it the air of an orchestrated hate campaign. Initially, Lewis and NME.com seemed to try and tough out the growing tide of criticism the tweet was generating. Ed didn't comment directly, but when fans raised the issue he posted neutral comments that alluded to the issue: 'It's cool, I'm just trying to be successful in my field making the music I want to make and working as hard as I can,' he wrote, along with 'You have to have a thick skin in this business.'

On 16 January 2012, Lewis and the *NME*'s website were forced to back down. It was less of an apology, more of an excruciating, extended grovel. 'Oh dear,' Lewis wrote. 'It's certainly not my goal in life to add to the sum total of bile and viciousness online. God knows there's enough of it already. That's why I cringe at the memory, and really, really wish I hadn't done it. Either in my name, or *NME*'s. For that reason I'd like to say sorry to Ed, who dealt with the whole thing with saint-like calm, as well as anyone who was upset by the insults that gushed forth. I'd also like to apologise to followers of @nmemagazine's twitter feed, who presumably signed up to be kept abreast of music news, not be subjected to the NME.com editor's slightly baffling personal tirade. It was a clanking great social media fail, and I'm thoroughly ashamed of myself.'

The *NME*'s readership seemed to be split between those who agreed with the original tweet, those who didn't and those who thought the website was a disgrace for having to back down in such a humiliating way. Sheeran's response to the apology – in reply to a tweet congratulating him on the way he had handled the situation – only served to cast Lewis and NME.com into an even worse light with its humble simplicity: 'Yeah, fair play, no hard feelings'.

It seemed almost supernaturally good-natured of Sheeran to react in this way. Something about the whole affair may have sparked something inside him, reminding him of incidents further in his past. Later, when asked by *The Guardian* about what happened, he likened the matter to being bullied at school: 'I've had worse, I went through school with this,' he said, pointing at his hair.

Back to the music. Valentine's Day saw the release of a new collaborative EP, this time with Yelawolf, a US rapper signed to Eminem's Shady Records alongside the likes of 50 Cent and D12. *The Slumdon Bridge* EP – a Sheeran pun if ever there was one – was a free download in this country and seemed aimed at giving Ed a connection with the US market. All four tracks were recorded in one session.

'What happened with Ed Sheeran was I got hit up and they said, "Hey, this kid Ed wants to do an EP,"' Yelawolf – aka Michael Atha – explained to Allhiphop.com. 'I was like, What's up with his music? I listened to his music and I was like, Damn this kid's music rips, but I don't know. I didn't really know how the music was going to come out, but I was just like, Fuck it, let's just get in the studio and see what happens. I literally pulled into LA and did the whole thing in one night,' he continued. 'We just vibed, man. That kid is something else. He plays guitar and sings and he raps. He's only 21 and it's amazing that some people just get it so young. He's just going to flourish as an artist, there's no telling where he's going to be in 10 years and he's doing classic shit right now.'

'I'm a big fan of Yelawolf,' Ed told Artistdirect.com. 'I got the opportunity to get in touch with him. I said, "I want to do a four-track project with you. Are you cool with that?" He said he was. We hooked up for ten hours in the studio and made four songs from scratch. He's into rock 'n' roll and punk music. I'm into folk music and shades of singer-songwriter stuff. We put all of our influences in a big bowl and mixed them. It was a new experience for all of us. It just happened. It came together well.'

To be fair, the EP is a mixed bag. The first track 'London Bridge' is an intriguing concoction of spaghetti western textures, swampy rap and Sheeran's variation on the popular nursery rhyme. It's interesting, but it doesn't leaving you aching for more. The quality picks up considerably with 'You Don't Know (For Fuck's Sake)', a loopy, late-night series of musings with Sheeran using the song to tell us where his life is currently at. 'Faces' allows Yelawolf to up the pace with rat-a-tat rhymes over industrial beats with Ed taking the lead on the multi-voiced chorus. The final track 'Tone' is synthy, sweary and short, and feels a little like filler culled from the closes stages of the recording session.

Longtime Sheeran supporters SB.TV were unsurprisingly keen on the project in their review. 'The four track EP has relative consistency, each track seamlessly flowing into the next – Yelawolf is impressive as ever, offering a range of spitting intensity whilst Ed keeps the beat together and takes control of the chorus – a very similar blueprint to *No.5 Collaborations Project* EP. Right now Ed is riding a wave, anything he puts out is likely to be well received because of his all round popularity. But he refuses to stay on one path, instead experimenting with this release. This underlines how Ed is sticking to his roots, his first five EP's were all of different genres and it looks as if he'll be using his wide range of talents for a wide range of musical output for a long time to come.'

'*Slumdon Bridge* is short and sweet and one can only hope that they release more music in tandem,' was the view from the Planet Ill website. 'This effort should definitely act as the American hip hop pipeline for the English music marvel. The kid is uber-talented and it's only a matter of time till he catches the ear of a hip hop heavyweight; as for Yelawolf, he continues to remind haters that Eminem signed him for a reason.

The Allhiphop website said: 'It's a unique project from start to finish, and it is well worth noting that Yelawolf and Ed Sheeran are talented enough to pull this off without seeming like a gimmick. It's the most unlikely of teams, but it works. Here's to hoping that we see more of them together in the future.'

Slumdon Bridge was just one of a dizzying series of collaborations, guest appearances and songwriting contributions that Sheeran would now be involved in alongside his regular releases. There was little or no consistency in terms of the style of music these releases offered, which appeared to be just the way Sheeran wanted it. 'Because the internet and iTunes have destroyed all genre barriers, no one gets into their set genres any more, they're just into all sorts of music,' he told Real Radio. 'Nowadays when you click on a Lady Gaga video on Viva and you get things coming up on the sidebar. Maybe my video comes up, or Knife Party or Vampire Weekend. No one cares about genres any more, they are just into really good music.'

Ed featured on the Wiley track 'If I Could' – though he didn't get to accompany the king of grime to Kingston, Jamaica for the video shoot – supplying lush, multi-tracked vocals to an otherwise minimalist track that's no more than a beat, a riff and Wiley's rhymes. DJ, mixer and producer Lew White put Ed more to the forefront on his track 'Young Guns', which also features Devlin, east London MC Griminal and singer Yasmin who'd toured with Ed when they both supported Example. For once, Ed took a leading role in the video to accompany the track. Despite this, the song only got to Number 86 in the UK charts – perhaps because there were just too many ingredients to make it truly memorable.

'Hush Little Baby' with Wretch 32 was another Sheeran appearance that failed to help create a sizable hit. It only managed to get to Number 35 in the singles chart, despite Ed's hefty vocal contribution and a fleeting appearance in the video. '(All Along the) Watchtower' with regular collaborator

Devlin saw Ed in sampling territory that would have taken him right back to those long car journeys from West Yorkshire to London. Featuring Ed singing the lead lines of the Bob Dylan song over the guitar riff from Jimi Hendrix's cover version, the track was accompanied by a full-on *Sweeney* style video. Playing against type, Sheeran was an unlikely looking bad guy, driving a getaway car while suffering from a gunshot wound to the gut.

Keeping it in the family, he also appeared on the track 'All Falls Down' for his cousin Jethro – aka Alonestar – alongside Rosie Ribbons, a former *Pop Idol* contestant. The song appeared on Alonestar's Warrior EP, released in March 2012.

Ed appeared on the track 'Suits' by London rapper Kasha Rae too. It's a terrific summery track with Ed explaining why, in a typical piece of Sheeran wordplay, suits don't suit him. But despite being up front in both the song and the accompanying video, Sheeran wasn't credited. 'You may be wondering why Ed's name has not been mentioned in the title,' Kasha Rae said in a statement. 'The truth is, I'm not being disrespectful to Ed but it's due to complex law of rights and ownerships that keep the music industry together. In most circumstances this track wouldn't of [sic] even been allowed to exist but Ed is a more fortunate artist than most and has a lot of control over what does and doesn't happen. However, as he is a good friend and we made this way before any contracts and lawyers got involved, we are able to release this new song to you as my debut for 2012. Hopefully we can make a mark, we might even make radio, TV and vevo. As you have probably seen on his Twitter, Ed is in full support of this music video's release and I cannot thank him enough for this. Thank you all, Ed and of course my real heads for your support. Big Big Love!'

While he didn't always get a credit as a performer, Ed's credit as a songwriter began to pop on a regular basis. He wrote a song called 'Il Sole Cade' for Italian pop star Carlo Alberto. Just to show how open he was to different artists using his songs, he also contributed a track to boy band One Direction, put together by Simon Cowell from odds and ends of contestants during the 2010 series of *The X Factor*. Ed already had an *X Factor* connection: he'd contributed to the song 'Love Shine Down', a light skanking track on the debut album of finalist Olly Murs. Murs's album had gone to Number 2 in the charts, but One Direction's success had gone through the roof.

Sheeran contributed the track 'Moments' to the deluxe edition of One Direction's debut *Up All Night*. 'I wrote that years ago,' he told News.com. 'I had a CD of 40 songs I was giving to publishers. Harry [Styles of One Direction] was staying at my guitarist's friend's house at the time. They were putting their album together and they didn't have enough songs. I said, "Here's a CD. If you want one of these songs, have it." And it got on the album. It was a song I was never going to use. To have it on a multi-platinum selling album is quite nice.'

The co-writer of 'Moments' was writer and producer Si Hulbert, who has worked with Sugababes and Ceelo Green and had previously had a hand in one of Sheeran's hidden gems, a song called 'Fall Down'.

Despite handing 'Moments' over to the Anglo Irish boy band, Ed was still keen to make sure it was looked after. 'I was actually there when they recorded. I played most of the instruments on it, it was exactly how I wanted it to be and I told them how to sing it,' he told the TV show *Access Hollywood*. 'I'm quite a control freak when it comes to that ... I'm like, this is how I want the song to be. I like their version.'

The song caused a stir because of internet rumours that its lyric was about suicide – worrying considering the age of many One Direction fans. Ed was keen to diffuse the claim: 'It's actually about my ex-girlfriend,' he stated. 'Not about suicide.'

As a result of the One Direction connection Ed formed an unlikely friendship with band member Harry Styles. 'Harry's a lad,' Ed told *In Demand*. 'When you're on the same promo run as someone or in the same kind of situation as someone you grow quite close, friendship-wise. He's a very cool guy. They're all really cool guys. If you take the boy band element out of it, they're just teenage dudes.'

In July 2012 Ed made another collaborative foothold in the US when he revealed he was writing with America's foremost pop star: Taylor Swift. She even released a video of her sitting on a kitchen floor duetting with Ed on 'Lego House'. 'Taylor is such a cool person, such a sweetheart, really like her,' Ed told *Access Hollywood*. 'One minute I was doing a gig in Nashville and her manager was there.

The next we were writing songs together. It was quite a quick process.'

Ed's 21st birthday was marked by the release of his next 'proper' single, 'Drunk'. As it happens, he spent part of the day loosening the ties on his normally strict personal regime. 'Thank you all so much for the birthday love!' he tweeted. 'Hope all of you lot have a wicked day. Mine is consisting of me breaking my drinking ban with a lot of [ultra strong Suffolk beer] Adnams Broadside.'

'Drunk' wasn't Ed's first choice for a single release at this stage, but unusually for him, he went with the flow. 'I've always wanted to release "Give Me Love",' he told the *Daily Record*. 'That was meant to be the fourth single but "Drunk" got play-listed before we put it to radio, so we kind of had to go with that.'

The single was accompanied by an 'on the road' video of backstage life, fan interaction and studio japes, put together by another of Sheeran's cousins, Murray Cummings. There was also a slicker, official version by Emil Nava that would see Ed centre stage in a video for the first time. 'With "The A Team", the song is a story so the video basically tells the story,' Ed explained to SB.TV. 'With "You Need Me" the song revolves around the lyrical aspect so I got Matt to do all the sign language. With "Lego House" it was like, how can you make it less commercial? With a freaky video with Harry Potter character being a stalker! "Drunk" was the first time I wanted to show a bit of a sense of humour and make something fun.'

In that spirit, Ed described the video to fans on Twitter

thus: 'Me appearing for the first time in a music video with some pussy... (cats)'

Ed explained the thrust of the video in slightly more detail to Capital FM: 'A cat takes me out and gets me drunk,' he said. 'There's basically a bit with a house party with the cats and these girls come back to the house party and hook up with some of the cats. It's really weird, and I just go a bit nuts.'

The cat in the video, incidentally, was in fact two cats – one of them a female called Dave. Both were much in demand 'acting cats' that had appeared in *James Bond*, *Harry Potter* and *Pirates of the Caribbean* films.

For the purposes of the filming, normally teetotal Ed had to play the part of the party boy: 'I break all the lights, I get a bottle of beer and I spray it all over the girls and afterwards I'm like, I'm really sorry. I totally soaked them from head to foot in beer. While we were filming it, the director's a bit kinda like bonks and he's very, very cool, but he was like, Ed, you just gotta go mental. I'm quite a reserved chilled guy, and he kept pushing me and pushing me and pushing me and just after a while I snapped and went nuts.'

The reason – in the video – that Ed is going nuts is because he's split with his girlfriend. Playing the part was teenage Scottish singer Nina Nesbitt. The 17-year-old from Balerno near Edinburgh had supported Sheeran in the past and it had just been announced that she would be on tour with him in Europe in March. It wasn't long before the press were linking the pair off screen as well. REVEALED:

CHART-TOPPER ED SHEERAN ENJOYS ROMANTIC HOLIDAY IN VENICE WITH SCOTTISH SINGER NINA NESBITT said the headline in Scotland's *Daily Record*, when the pair were spotted in Italy. 'They could be any pair of young lovers in the world's most romantic city,' the story said. 'Dressed down and wrapped up against the winter chill, the couple strolled through the squares and by the canals of Venice hand-in-hand. But few onlookers who saw them gazing into each other's eyes over lunch would have realised the woolly hat-wearing young man is a chart-topping star. And that probably suited "A Team" singer Ed Sheeran down to the ground as he enjoyed a peaceful Italian break with his new love, 17-year-old Scot Nina Nesbitt.'

The paper also pounced on tweets the pair had sent in December: 'Had a lovely three hour phone conversation last night,' Ed had written online. Meanwhile, Nina had tweeted: 'I'm all smiley and nobody knows why' and: 'Loves waking up with a smile.'

Both Sheeran and Nesbitt's managers refused to comment on the stories, but that didn't stop the press writing about Ed and Nina as a couple: even *The Guardian* began to refer to Nesbitt as 'Ed Sheeran's other half'. That tabloid favourite, a 'source' told the *Daily Record*: 'In the past few weeks, Nina has spent quite a lot of time with Ed at his flat in London. It must be getting quite serious as he whisked her away to Venice.'

As she was just getting her career underway, Nesbitt had to start steeling herself for a 'How's your relationship with Ed going?' line of questioning in every interview. 'We're more just friends than anything else,' Nina later told journalist Beverley Lyons. 'We are just close. I let people think what they want.'

Nesbitt's association with Sheeran clearly did her no harm. In June 2012 it was announced that she'd signed a major deal with Universal. She'd be working with several songwriters on her debut album. One person in particular would be involved: Ed's right hand man Jake Gosling.

ELEVEN

NO REHAB
JUST YET

'I'm really bad at this...' Ed Sheeran said, standing on the vast stage, wearing an expensive-looking but slightly too tight suit. On 21 February 2012, Ed was at the O2 Arena in London. In his hand was a red, white and blue figurine – a BRIT award for Best British Male Solo Artist. Just four days after his 21st birthday he'd beaten the likes of Noel Gallagher, Professor Green and James Morrison to win it; now names tumbled out of his mouth in a list of thank yous.

The huge audience cheered him wildly – they clearly love an underdog. But there was more to come. Before long Ed had to return to the stage to pick up a second award, this time for British Breakthrough Act. Second time around, his speech was more succinct and he thanked the man he'd forgotten to mention last time around: his manager, Stuart Camp. 'He's the person who took me from a spotty, chubby, ginger teenager, to up here tonight,' Ed told the O2 crowd. Unable to resist the chance to make a private joke he added: 'So Stuart, lots of love, and... you need a new sofa.' The joke was a reference to the place the young man had called home for the past few years: his manager's settee.

'I'm ecstatic that what I did last year was recognised a little bit,' Ed later told BBC Radio Manchester when asked about his awards success. 'It means a lot to me, because it means a lot more to the fans, if that makes any sense. Awards are big congratulations for the year that you've had – and I'd say that the year that I've had was down to my fan base.'

Ed performed live at the BRITS that night – he changed out of the suit to play in his usual jeans and a t-shirt. His music teacher from Thomas Mills School in Framlingham was watching the ceremony at home, listening to the young man he'd taught just five years earlier. 'I watched him on the BRIT awards and he was clearly quite nervous,' Richard Hanley told me, 'and he sang with his guitar in this big venue – he seemed a bit vulnerable. Then you've got the likes of Adele and all the paraphernalia that went with her performance. Then Blur finished it all off with pyrotechnics and all sorts of stuff. And there's Ed with just his guitar... on his own.'

In March, Ed took his guitar to Austin, Texas to play at the South by Southwest festival. Though it also acts as a film and interactive technology festival, SXSW mainly acts as a showcase for emerging music stars. The careers of James Blunt and John Mayer were kick-started at the festival in previous years and Ed was clear as to why he was appearing. 'This is my first proper step into the US market,' he told *Forbes* magazine. 'I was actually meant to be here last year, and then I ended up getting signed and making a record. So I missed out on it. I play the music that I've always played, and it stood out enough in England to sell a few records, so hopefully it'll stand out here. I've got bright red hair, so I guess I stand out anyway.'

Although he had yet to release a single 'physical' piece of music in the States, Ed clearly had America in his sights. 'I'm happy to be in America and start off at the bottom,' he told Rap Up TV. 'To be given the opportunity to do it is the hardest part.' Adele was making waves in the US market by this time – could Sheeran be the next big thing in this new British invasion? 'We've been swapping acts for years. You gave us Hendrix and Dylan, we gave you The Beatles and the Stones,' he said. 'Now we're swapping again. We give you Tinie [Tempah], you give us Lil Wayne. We give you Adele, you give us Rihanna.'

Ed played a variety of showcase gigs at the SXSW event, included one sponsored by celebrity blogger Perez Hilton, who would become a major Sheeran cheerleader. He also performed a headlining a gig in support of his old friends at The Bedford in London, who were out in Texas promoting their venue. 'It was really critical to us to get a headliner on the show,' The Bedford's Tony Moore told me. 'Even though his career had been intertwined with us in the preceding years, priorities come into your life when you have success. So for him to take time out and do that for us was great.

'The audience loved him. I hadn't seen him for over a year in performance mode ... and success has turned him into an artist with an unbelievable capacity to entertain, to motivate and to fill a space with energy all on his own. What he did in Texas was show that one man with a small guitar and a looping pedal can take any size space and make it like a front room. He is the real deal.'

One thing happened that night that bears out Tony Moore's opinion: when Ed's set for The Bedford overran until 2am the venue – The Creekside at the Hilton Garden Inn – turned off the power and shut the gig down. Undeterred, Ed pulled out that old folkie trick from one of his earliest London gigs, stood on a table and sang 'Lego House' without amplification. The audiences at SXSW events have often seen it all before, but as Sheeran hit the last chord of the song, one audience member could be clearly heard giving her opinion: 'Wow!'

Back home, one performance by Ed Sheeran was on a less dramatic scale, but was no less important and probably more so. Aged just 14, Abigail Fleming from Maltby in Yorkshire had been told she had terminal cancer. She'd made a list of things she wanted to do before she died: a party to mark the 16th birthday that she would sadly never see, a hot air balloon ride, a stay at the Alton Towers Hotel, a trip to Scotland and a huge custard pie and jelly fight. She also wanted to see Ed Sheeran play live.

In February 2012 Ed travelled to the Bluebell Wood Children's Hospice in Sheffield, where Abigail was spending her last weeks and played for her at her bedside. 'He didn't just make her day, it made her life,' Abigail's mum Maria told the *Worksop Guardian*. 'It was his only day off. He flew in from Paris to London and then caught the train to Sheffield. Abigail gave him a card and a key ring to say thank you. He gave her a bracelet that somebody had given him for his 18th birthday, which I now wear. He was a complete gentleman and she really loved it.'

Some of Ed's performance for Abigail was videoed by her family. 'Any song you want to hear? I'm here for you,' Ed told the girl as she lay on her bed. With his guitar case open by his side, Sheeran played songs to Abigail from a chair next to her bed as she held a favourite soft toy. He played 'Lego House' and 'The A-Team'. When he got to the final lines of the song, it's almost as if he hadn't realised the resonance the words have until they came out of his mouth: '...for angels to die...'

'She was so caring and always put everyone else before herself,' Abigail's dad Richard later said. 'I told her I would swap places with her and she said, "No, that would mean [her brother] Aiden wouldn't have a dad." She made an impression on everyone.'

Clearly impressed by the work at Bluebell Wood, Ed decided to raise money for the hospice that looked after

Abigail. 'I'm gonna auction off all the Lego I've ever made and give the proceeds to charity,' he said on Twitter. 'Anyone wanna buy some Lego? It's all stuff I've made backstage at gigs, or the day my Album went #1, I made the Millennium Falcon, Hogwarts Castle. I'll set up the auction in 2 weeks once I've got all the models together and I'm home.'

Abigail Fleming died on 3 April 2012. Ed's response was typically low key: 'Rest in peace Abigail. My love and thoughts are with the family,' he posted online.

* * *

In March, Ed had announced that his next single would be 'Small Bump'. The video was again directed by Emil Nava and this time Ed is visible the whole time. It's essentially one long tracking shot of Ed sitting in a hospital waiting room as other patients fade in and out of vision in slow motion; a far more gentle affair than usual, designed to fit the downbeat mood of the song. 'The song's kind of hard hitting,' Nava told SB.TV, 'so I didn't want it to be too full on.' Perhaps unsurprisingly, as the fifth single released from an album that already contained previously released material, 'Small Bump' was Ed's least successful single to date, peaking at Number 25 in the UK charts.

In many ways, there was a bigger prize on the horizon: Sheeran's assault on America was being lined up. His record company was shouting out the news very loudly indeed: ED

SHEERAN TO BRING + TO AMERICA; U.K. SUPERSTAR TO HERALD RECORD-BREAKING DEBUT ALBUM WITH MAJOR NORTH AMERICAN TOUR ALONGSIDE SNOW PATROL was the headline from his US record company's press statement. The album + was now scheduled for a 12 June release in the States and Ed already had a performance slot on NBC's *Jimmy Fallon Show* booked in.

The hook-up with Snow Patrol came about by chance. Ed was travelling from Switzerland to Germany to play a gig when he spotted lead singer Gary Lightbody on the same plane. They noticed each other, but Sheeran noticed a 'shocked' look on Lightbody's face. 'I got in [to the venue] and there was a letter waiting for me and it was from Gary and he said, "The reason I looked so shocked before was that I had earphones in and I was listening to your album and I think it's great,"' Ed told the BBC. '"Come and have a drink with us later."' Over the drink, Lightbody invited Ed to support the band on their upcoming European tour. When he told the singer he couldn't because he was already committed to his own tour, Lightbody said: 'You might as well come on our American tour then.'

It was Ed's first serious inroad into the US market: 'It allows me to go to every single territory in America and do all the radio stations, which is one of the most important things to do if you're going to break there. It's a great step.'

Unsurprisingly, Ed already had a formula worked out that he thought would help him succeed in generating success in the US: 'Tour, tour, tour. Radio,' was the list of priorities he outlined in an interview with Globalgrind website. 'I'm going to release some really interesting music first for free. I think the music I've created is quite odd, and people are going to start talking about that. And then come with the first single, come with the second single, come with the album, and then just keep rolling out singles.'

The tour with Snow Patrol began on 29 March in Orlando, Florida. Ed was pleased to see that his favourite Robinson's Fruit and Barley drink had been provided for him backstage. He was also pleased to see that many fans at the front of the stage knew all the words to his songs. Everything was going perfectly. Sheeran was happy to be playing a swift 35-minute opening set for the easy-going rock band at nearly 30 shows. He also revealed he'd been writing songs with the band to go on the follow up to +. 'I've done around 20 new songs for the new album and I've been writing a lot with the Snow Patrol boys as well,' he told Perez Hilton. 'I knew them before so yeah, I was kind of friends with them, but I've written a song with them, so it's good.'

Life on the road with Snow Patrol seemed to agree with him. He got a snowflake tattoo to mark how important the tour was to his career and he and Lightbody were having fun. 'We played in Las Vegas, and Gary was given, I think, $1,000 in chips for playing a gig, and he didn't want to gamble, so he gave it to me,' Sheeran told the Popcrush website. 'And I gambled away $1,000 of Gary's money. I won $1,500 dollars, but then I lost it. The problem is they give out free drinks ... You get trigger happy.'

As the tour continued, so did the Snow Patrol/Sheeran love-in. Lead singer Gary Lightbody described Ed as a 'brother' to the band. 'He's the complete pop star,' Lightbody wrote on his blog. 'He will make smart, touching, soulful, powerful music for years to come and grow with every step and his fans will grow with him.'

As far as Sheeran was concerned, the feeling was mutual: 'The tour has been great,' Ed told the Soundspike website. 'I'm having the best time seeing America and playing in front of different crowds every night, and the Snow Patrol lads are so nice as well.'

But after a show in Phoenix on 14 May, with four days till the end of the tour, it was announced that Sheeran was heading home. 'Hope everyone understands, lots of love... So sorry to cancel, have to get home for personal reasons.'

Gary Lightbody: 'After Phoenix we bid Ed Sheeran a fond but sad farewell,' he wrote in a blog post. 'He has lit up the tour and our lives. He already rules the UK charts. He will rule the world by the end of the year. I guarantee it. A phenom he may be but not without good reason. He gets pop star level adulation and hero worship but what stands him apart from other 'pop stars' is that there is no one pulling his strings in the shadows. No Svengali writing his songs and telling him what to wear. Everything he has done, he has done on his own terms and all his songs are his own.'

The British press were all over the story but within a few hours, the tone of the coverage changed dramatically, suggesting that there were darker reasons for pulling out of the final shows. 'Apparently, media are running a story tomorrow about how I'm coming home early to enter rehab,' Ed tweeted. 'I'm missing four days of a tour to see my family. But yeah, no rehab just yet, but I am going to Legoland in a few weeks, so might need it after that.'

It's quite possible that Sheeran fanned the flames of the story by making the denial so early. He later explained why he did it to the BBC's *Newsbeat*: 'It was just making clear that I'm not entering rehab which was speculated. That's fair enough. I'm lucky enough to have the best job in the world. I travel the world and make people happy by playing music. There's no chance of burning out whilst doing that. It's a brilliant job. I'm not a very interesting person publicly so there isn't a lot to write about me.'

Although it was well known that Ed favoured a glass of Robinson's squash over alcohol these days, he had previously made his views on drugs clear. 'I won't go down the wrong path, I'm not that kind of guy,' he told the *Daily Record* in 2011. 'I'm not a drug-taker. Most of the people I've met on coke are idiots. They just talk too much and I wouldn't want to subject someone to me being like that because I talk too much anyway.'

All of Sheeran's statements showed immense patience and good humour – particularly when put in the context of what had really happened. Ed's beloved granddad Bill was becoming increasingly frail and concern about his health was enough for Ed to make the decision to come home and go to Ireland. 'I had to leave to go and see my granddad,' he later told *Access Hollywood*. 'I missed four dates to come home early. The press were ringing up to say why are you coming home?' Ed decided to keep the truth quiet so his extended family didn't find out about the situation in the newspapers. 'I've got 30 cousins on my granddad's side and I didn't want them reading it in the press. So I didn't say anything. The next day there was a story saying I was going into rehab. I had school friends ringing me up saying, "You alright?"'

Ed kept a low profile in Ireland for the next few days, but he broke cover on 17 May to go to the Grosvenor House Hotel in London to accept an Ivor Novello Award for 'The A Team', which had been voted Best Song Musically and Lyrically. The prestigious awards, presented by the British Academy of Songwriters, Composers and Authors, have been given out since 1955 to recognise songwriting talent; previous winners include Sheeran favourites like Sir Elton John, John Lennon and Coldplay. The award was presented to him by singer songwriter David Gray, an acoustic artist cut from very similar cloth to Sheeran. 'I'm happy,' Ed told Capital FM. 'I'm a bit emotional to be honest. It's the one award you always dream about as a songwriter so to get it first time round, off someone that I started [in] music listening to, it's sweet.'

Not everyone was quite so pleased with Sheeran's win. Ed's old adversaries at NME.com ran a blog by journalist

Matthew Horton under the headline: 'Is Ed Sheeran's "The A Team" Really 2011's Best Song?' Branding the song musically ordinary and lyrically heavy-handed, the website questioned whether Sheeran had any business being nominated, let alone winning. 'The category for Best Song Musically and Lyrically is where the real prestige lies, parsing songs down to their bare bones and honouring the one that, presumably, shows up flawless,' Horton wrote. 'This year it's Ed Sheeran's "The A Team". That can't be right, can it? Previous winners like Amy Winehouse's "Love Is A Losing Game", Elbow's "One Day Like This" and even Will Young's "Leave Right Now" throw "The A Team" victory into stark relief. Those are songs with real emotional heft, surprises and hooks that dig into your hippocampus like a velvet scalpel. Even this year there were more worthy candidates. Fellow nominees Adele's "Rolling in the Deep" and Florence + The Machine's "Shake It Out" are surely stronger.'

This time, the *NME*'s online swipe at Sheeran didn't have the same impact; perhaps he was getting too big for their jibes to have any effect. As Ed later put it on Twitter: 'Success is the best revenge for anything. Keep ya head down and work hard to achieve.'

As if to bear this out, at the end of May it was confirmed that + had gone quadruple platinum in the UK – 1.2 million people had bought a copy of the album. More proof that Sheeran was pulling away from the influence of critics came a few days later when Ed performed at the Queen's Diamond Jubilee Concert at Buckingham Palace. As he stood on the specially constructed stage it must surely have crossed his mind that just a few years earlier, he'd slept rough a few yards from where he was now performing to a billion people.

'It was an honour to play the Queen's Jubilee and such an honour to be part of that line up,' Ed told *Access Hollywood*. 'Going on stage at the end and singing with Paul McCartney and having Stevie Wonder behind me while we're doing the National Anthem and him playing the harmonica, it was such a surreal experience. Grace Jones told me I looked like her granddaughter – which was a compliment.'

After the show he was introduced to The Queen by Kylie Minogue – now *there's* something that doesn't happen every day. 'There's a funny picture of me shaking [The Queen's] hand and she looks very happy, but in reality she didn't see my set, she didn't know who I was. It was like (adopts very posh accent), "Helloooo, how are yoooo..." I'm like, yeah what's going on? Happy Jubilee!'

Ed also took the opportunity to have his picture taken with Prince Harry backstage. In Rupert Grint's absence, Ed and the Prince are surely two out of the three of the world's most high profile gingers. 'We do look very similar,' Ed said of his royal photo opportunity.

Ed's parents were with him backstage and mum Imogen was particularly thrilled to meet Ms Minogue. 'They were in the corner for ages, talking away,' Ed told *The Sun*. 'I just stood there while they talked, thinking about how surreal it was. We didn't leave until the early hours. My mum loved it, though. I took both my parents and this is something that has made them actually be happy with me being a musician now, performing with Paul McCartney and meeting The Queen.'

In fact McCartney would provide Ed with the highlight of the night – in many ways, the highlight of his whole year. 'I got to introduce my dad to Paul McCartney, that was quite a cool moment,' he told BBC East. 'My dad's been listening to The Beatles for years. I'd met Paul earlier in the evening. My dad was standing with me and Paul brought his grandson over to say "hi" to me – so I got the opportunity to say, "Dad meet Paul... Paul meet Dad."'

Many reviewers were scathing about the quality of the acts at the event – some of the old stagers came in for harsh criticism for the quality of their singing. Ed Sheeran, for many, was a highlight: 'Amidst all the showbiz razzmatazz, singer-songwriter Ed Sheeran looked and sounded oddly out of place delivering a tender acoustic performance of "The A Team", a ballad about prostitution and drugs,' said the *Daily Telegraph*. 'It was like an outbreak of authenticity at a camp cabaret. In a lifetime of attending these kind of events, this may count as the most unusual acts the Queen has ever seen.'

Appearing at the event brought things full circle for Ed. As an 11-year-old he'd watched the Golden Jubilee concert on TV – seeing Eric Clapton play had made him want to take up the guitar – and many of the acts who'd played a decade earlier like Sir Elton John and Sir Tom Jones were there again that night. 'It was a pretty nice experience. I took up the guitar the day after I watched the Jubilee concert ten years ago. I started after seeing Eric Clapton – I can't believe I am here ten years later.'

TWELVE

DRIVEN

As the summer of 2012 got underway there were major UK events on Ed's schedule. Although he was at the stage where he could easily sell out UK arenas, he held back, concerned that his connection with the audience would be lost if the spaces he performed in became too big. 'I'm not an arena act yet,' he told the BBC. 'If you go and see Rihanna at an arena it fits. If you go and see a scruffy little ginger kid with a guitar on a stage it isn't going to work. I wouldn't want to cheat fans out of money just to sell more tickets. I'm more than happy. On the next tour I'm doing five [nights at the] Hammersmith Apollo, which is 25,000 tickets, as opposed to [playing the] O2 arena which is 17,000 tickets. I'm playing to more people than I would be doing arenas, but it's in a more intimate environment and they can walk away from the thing thinking they have something from the gig, rather than that they saw a spectacle. I'm not a spectacle yet, I'm an intimate act. When I'm a spectacle, then I'll go to arenas.'

But major festivals and outdoor events were still to Ed's taste. On 8 June 2012 he played at RockNess, at Dores on the banks of Loch Ness in Scotland. He caused something of a stir after deciding to take the train up to Inverness on his own; bemused railway staff couldn't believe he wasn't travelling first class. Given that he was by the now just about the most recognisable musician in Britain it's not surprising he was swamped by fans, many of whom seemed to treat the red-haired Sheeran as an honorary Scot. 'I love Scotland. Scotland's a very special place for me and I can't wait to go and play there,' Ed told Scottish newspaper the *Daily Record*. 'The crowds are always brilliant to me. I'm ready to look for the monster. I'm going skinny dipping in Loch Ness.'

Ed popped up earlier in the day during Wretch 32's set, but it was his headlining appearance that caught the attention of the reviewers. *The Guardian* said: 'The first true lift-off moment of the festival came halfway through Ed Sheeran's set, when the affable Brit winner speed-coached an overflowing second-stage tent into an unexpected but effective gospel choir.'

'Last May he was dutifully playing to a couple of hundred in Glasgow's ABC2,' said STV. 'Just over a year later he's commanding a crowd of thousands with ease. It's some rise in fortune for this year's award-laden musician of the moment, and he handles it rather beautifully, without any betrayal of ego, easily getting a good old singalong going for "Drunk" - the title alone guaranteeing a crowd reception usually reserved for royalty.'

Unsurprisingly, there was one dissenting voice. 'RockNess, set on the banks of the stunning Loch Ness, an ideal weekend for raucous naughtiness,' said NME.com. 'Frustratingly, there's little on offer on Friday to turn this fest into the big-rave orgy it'll later become. Instead we're left with a snot-nosed Ed Sheeran to entertain us.'

It was the American market that Ed was aiming to entertain when + was finally released in the States on 12 June. Sheeran spent the day promoting the album, starting with an early morning performance of 'The A Team' on NBC's *Today* show. He told US website Soundspike that he was willing to put in the work to break the American market: 'The US is a market that UK artists rarely break into because it's so massive, and to be honest, you've already got 15 artists like our big ones, apart from the obvious like Adele. But it's such a major market to have, so I'm prepared to do everything I can to achieve long-lasting success here.'

It's believed that Sheeran had put aside nine months to crack the States. He needn't have bothered. On the day of its release + went to Number 1 on the US iTunes chart. Then it did the same in Canada: 'Oh my word!!' Ed tweeted. 'My album is -#1 on USA iTunes!!!! So happy right now. And Canada!!! Getting emotional right now, gonna eat some nachos.'

The album sold 42,000 copies in its first week – 79 per cent were downloads – sending it to Number 5 on the US *Billboard* chart, which also takes into account radio airplay. The album's performance on both charts seemed to take even Sheeran by surprise: 'The reception for my album differed in the States from the UK because in the UK I'd had two hit singles and a third one that was getting radio play before the album came out,' Ed told Billboard.com. '[We had] a lot of pre-orders and very good touring so we knew it was going to chart, we knew it was going to sell, it was a question of how much. In America I haven't had a hot single at all – there was no preconception at all as to where the album would go. As soon as it went live on iTunes it went straight to Number 1. It was a real shock moment.'

The chart placing for + was the highest debut on *Billboard* for a British solo artist since Susan Boyle's *I Dreamed a Dream* became a Christmas hit in 2009. Despite this Sheeran was still cagey, perhaps wary that breaking the US might be seen to be coming too quickly, too easily – he was in for the long run. 'There's a tiny bit to celebrate now but not enough to warrant celebrating loads,' he told Digital Spy. 'I don't want to get blinded by a small bit of success. Until the album sells a million copies there won't be a lot to celebrate. I've played some of my first shows out there and they've gone down well, but there's still a long way to go. I've done a lot for the next record. The writing and recording thing comes in bursts. I'm still growing up, and I'd like to say this album is a little bit more mature, but it's probably not! It's probably what people are expecting from me. If they like me, then they'll like it!'

He also hinted that now was the time to take himself away from the UK, fearing perhaps that he was in danger of becoming overexposed: 'I spent the last five years in the UK – I've done four tours and it's almost come to the end of my album cycle. I think people will be expecting me to go away for a while anyway. I think people would get a bit sick of me if I didn't take a break!'

Throughout the remainder of June, Sheeran would maintain a staggering work rate: Minneapolis, Denver, San Francisco, Toronto, France, Germany, Norway, Italy, Switzerland and Belgium. The itinerary was so intense that one airline managed to lose two of Sheeran's beloved Martin guitars. 'So after Delta messing up the flight over here [to France], they have lost both my guitars,' he tweeted. 'Bring back Cyril and Nigel. Hope I get them back in time for Hackney weekend.'

Cyril and Nigel were found later that day – 'safe and sound' – and it was Nigel that Ed had in his hand as he took to the stage of the Hackney Weekend. He played a 40-minute set at the Radio 1 event – just five songs stretched and looped into a blur of audience participation, lighters and mobile phones in the air and call-and-response showmanship. Throughout the set, Ed asked for the audience to shout two words back at him. They did it each time without question. The words in question were ... 'Hell yeah!'

As well as the upfront charms of Jay-Z, Rihanna and

Nicki Minaj, the Radio 1 Hackney Weekend also saw a different kind of performer take to the various stages: Jessie Ware, Delilah, Emeli Sandé and Ben Howard. All are low key, thoughtful, soul-tinged performers with roots appeal and a touch of the hippy about them. All perhaps beneficiaries of the 'Ed Sheeran effect'. It's hard to imagine the likes of Radio 1 having anything to do with someone like Ben Howard before Sheeran opened the field up. Indeed, Sheeran has professed himself a fan of Howard and urged his fans to buy Howard's debut album *Every Kingdom*. Howard uses the guitar-tapping technique similar to the one Sheeran studied with Preston Reed and his vocals are straight out of the Damien Rice school of sensitivity via the John Martyn college of slurred singing. Indeed, Howard namechecks the late Martyn with the same vigour that Sheeran mentions Rice. Howard told journalist Ruth Carruthers in 2009: 'John Martyn's the boy. He's really the complete songwriting package. I don't think there are many people who come close to his musicality and passion, he's a real heart on his sleeve type of guy and I really admire that. May he rest in peace.'

Music of the early 1970s – the music of John and Imogen Sheeran's record collection – has come out of the shadows thanks to Ed Sheeran. For a long time, music from this period – acoustic, well meaning, brown bread, singer-songwriter music – was consigned to the section at the back of the popular culture store marked 'unfashionable' since punk came along in 1976. History was re-written in the 1970s and many traces and strains of music were airbrushed away by music writers embarrassed by their own slightly beardy record collections. It's an attitude adopted wholeheartedly by the likes of the *NME* at the time and perhaps goes some way to explaining the paper's antipathy towards Sheeran now. Ed seems to have skipped a generation, bypassing many of the references that musicians and critics usually hold dear and taking his lead from the music he heard while travelling in his parents' car from West Yorkshire to London. Sheeran has made it OK to hark back to a time before punk; the irony is that he's the most 'punk' musician this country has produced for decades. The DIY attitude, the independent releases, the lack of compromise, the sign-a-deal-on-my-own-terms stance: very punk. The way he's presented himself is punk too: the everyman, the person you could see in a shopping centre anywhere in the land. Ed Sheeran: the anti-rockstar. 'I'd like to convey the image of being just a regular person rather than being very glossy,' he told BBC Blast. 'I'd like to look like someone's kids or someone's mate or someone's brother, rather than someone you wouldn't ever meet.'

The kind of acts that are coming through now, perhaps due to Sheeran's success, also have something of a disregard for genres, labels and musical barriers. Ironically, there's even been an attempt to put a label on this new breed and plonk Sheeran as its figurehead. The *Daily Telegraph* dubbed them 'The New Hip Hop Troubadours', pulling in artists like Plan B, Maverick Sabre and – rather confusingly – Lana Del Rey. In the *Telegraph* article, journalist Neil McCormick tried very hard to flag up a new 'movement' where, essentially there wasn't one, but it was a reasonable attempt to make sense of something that seemed to be an anomaly.

'Something is changing in the rarefied world of the sensitive singer-songwriter,' he wrote. 'Those tremulous bards who strum acoustic guitars and wax poetic about their deepest feelings. Listen closely and you will hear influences creeping in from a genre of music not particularly celebrated for sensitivity or melodiousness. Urban beats and the hyperactive lyrical flow of rap are blending with the introspective balladry and loaded emotions of strumming troubadours. Among a new wave of singer-songwriters, Eminem and Jay-Z are as likely to be cited as an influence as Bob Dylan and Joni Mitchell. Hip hop has wound its way from the streets to the bedsits. Poster boy for this new rapport is Ed Sheeran... At first sight Sheeran seems an anachronism in the modern hit parade, plucking his acoustic and singing of drug addicts ("The A Team") and lost love ("Lego House"), until you pay attention to the way he delivers a line, switching seamlessly from soft crooning to quick-fire, double-time blasts packed with internal rhymes and lyrics that flow across verse breaks with the grandstanding metres and cadences of rap.'

Talk of 'movements' and 'new rapports' is rather quaint in this day and age. It worked in the late 1970s and 1980s when journalists needed labels to apply to acts to generate interest and newspaper sales. In a cross-referenced, net-led, iPodded world that no longer applies. But it's too simplistic to suggest that if you bang something on the internet and fire off a couple of tweets, it will sell. Sheeran for one believes it's a generational thing and that the oldies in the mainstream media just don't get it: 'That's what the media want it to be,' he told the *Daily Telegraph* when asked if his success has been purely an internet phenomenon. 'Because I don't think they can work out how it happened. I can record in a studio, eight tracks for a grand, then pay 60 dollars to have it distributed worldwide on iTunes and Spotify, shoot a video for twenty quid, and put that on YouTube and post it on Facebook, and people will see it, so in a sense it's a social media thing, but there's a lot that goes with it.'

There's no doubt that Ed is one of the first British acts to be part of and a product of the digital, multi-platform age. If proof was needed, he was named as the most streamed act of 2011 by the Official Chart Company, beating the likes of Rihanna, Coldplay and David Guetta. The figures were compiled by combining plays on sites Spotify, Napster and Deezer. But Sheeran seems slightly niggled by the idea that he is purely a product of the net and social media, as if it negates all that hard work he has put in. 'I don't necessarily think it was all to do with the amount of followers I had on Twitter or the YouTube following I had,' he told the BBC. 'I think a lot of my career is to do with the internet and I think I've used it to my advantage. I've put videos up and spoken to people on Twitter and updated on Facebook but I think the main thing to break through is to release consistently good music that you're happy with and back it with live shows. That's the way to do it.'

The 'way to do it' appears to be good old-fashioned hard work. 'When I switch off I feel like I'm being lazy,' Sheeran confessed to *The Sun*. 'My family tell me to slow down but, ultimately, they understand.'

The other thing that seems to ruffle Sheeran's feathers is a sense that he's in some way a fluke and that he's just got lucky. 'I don't believe in luck as a rule,' he pointed out in an interview with OurVinyl TV. 'Luck is circumstance, how you put yourself in certain positions and how you work yourself in or out of those positions. Luck is a mixture between work ethic, circumstance and people helping you. I've been lucky to come across some very nice people, but if I hadn't been doing three gigs a night maybe I wouldn't have bumped into those people. It's all relative.'

Ed Sheeran has definitely worked himself into the position he now occupies and if the bottom ever falls out of the hip hop troubadour market, he could always make a living as a motivational speaker for business leaders – never give up, do it on your own terms, learn from your failures, success is its own reward. These are the attitudes and principles he seems to live by and they'd sit just as easily with a captain of industry as they would a singer with an undersized guitar.

Sheeran's work ethic has been, and continues to be, a little bit frightening. Even those who don't care for Sheeran's music can't fault the amount of work he's put into getting it out to as many people as possible. He is Mr Motivated, to an almost chilling degree. But, as Ed himself puts it: 'No one is going to do it for you.' His work ethic has brought him quadruple platinum status in Britain, and now success in America. He has now joined the likes of Adele, One Direction and The Wanted as part of a pop culture raiding party, pillaging the US charts and displacing their home grown acts. We haven't seen a British invasion like this since MTV propelled the image-savvy Brit bands of the early 1980s – Culture Club, The Police, Duran Duran – into the US charts. Sheeran now forms part of an elite and diverse UK brigade of young musicians and singers who have taken the States off guard and by storm.

Sheeran seems to like the American way of life and their attitude towards success: 'The outlook on life in America is so much different to England,' he told News.com. 'In England if a guy had gone from nothing to something, lived in a big house, married a beautiful woman and drove a Ferrari, people wouldn't like it. In America that's celebrated. It's quite refreshing coming to a country where I haven't really done anything yet and they celebrate my success. I am my worst critic. I think that's healthy. I'm very underwhelmed by myself. It's not like I'm thinking, I've sold a million albums in England, I'm smashing it. I think, I've sold a million albums in England and about 200 in America. There's a lot more work to do.'

Is this a strong work ethic – or control freakery? One of the reasons Sheeran decided to be a solo performer rather than a member of a group is because he could be in complete control of what he did and the way he did it – plus he knew he'd never quit. 'If I said I was going to do something, I would do it,' he told *Total Guitar*. 'Whereas with a band, one person can be like that and another person can be, "Actually, I would prefer to go back to school and get a degree." It's a lot easier being solo.'

Sheeran's desire to stay in control extends to his Facebook page. In June 2012 a posting about his songwriting activities with other performers was made without his knowledge. Ed's response was swift and left no one in any doubt that he was in charge of all aspects of his career: 'I'm taking control of this page again, starting to piss me off not having full control on here,' he wrote. 'I have always said I will do what I want musically, whether it be making songs with underground rappers, or writing songs for pop acts, or doing my own solo thing. I love making music, if you are a fan of me you will understand that. I am always gonna continue making good music for myself, collaborating with my favourite artists, and as far as songwriting is concerned, I will write for who I want. I just enjoy writing songs. Hope this has cleared things up for anyone who was confused. I'm back to running this page, no one else. Ello. Ed x.'

After a summer of travels, on 12 July 2012 Ed Sheeran returned to his adopted home of Suffolk to play a gig in the beautiful surroundings of High Lodge in Thetford Forest. The forest – which is so large it stretches into neighbouring Norfolk – is normally home to mountain bikers and day trippers, but in recent years has staged Forestry Commission-sponsored gigs by the likes of Ed's hero Van Morrison and the man he tried to out-gig, James Morrison.

The 8,000 tickets for the show went on sale in January. Within minutes they had all been snapped up by local fans, perhaps sensing that his success would take him away from the place where he grew up and played his first ever gigs. 'Thetford Forest gig sold out in 25 minutes this morning J,' he tweeted. 'Can't ask for more than that. Love you all.'

As he took to the stage he was greeted by a sea of fans of all ages. Little children were held aloft by their parents, teenage girls in pawprint hoodies screamed and their boyfriends held camera phones aloft to record the proceedings. 'It's good to be home,' he said as he launched into his first song 'Give Me Love', the track from + that he believes is the best indicator of where he's heading next. As he stamps on his effects pedal to create a backing loop of guitar, he talks to the audience. 'Hello, my name is Ed and my job for the next two hours is to entertain you. Your job is to be entertained.'

According to the *East Anglian Daily Times*, the paper that has tracked his progress from the start, he did just that. 'Musically speaking, the Framlingham boy who once played more than 300 gigs in a year has become a man,' the paper's review said the following morning. 'His appeal, in these days of pyrotechnics and razzle dazzle, lies in his simplicity. There are no holograms, explosions or scantily clad dancers with Ed. Instead, it's just him and his guitar alone on stage. It's more than enough. In his hands, the simple instrument and his voice – pitch perfect, by the way – seemed to fill the forest arena far better than a bigger and louder band ever could. Thousands of fans singing along to every word helped, of course, and at times the gig took on a festival feel – apt given the fact that Latitude is just down the road this weekend. Of course, singing is not all Ed does – the 21-year-old can also turn his sickeningly talented hand to rapping and beatboxing with great aplomb, and he duly did so to a rapturous reception. Welcome home, Ed. Next time, don't leave it so long.'

'Have to say,' Ed tweeted the morning after the show,' Thetford was one of the highlights of my career. I love being home.' But given the way his career is now heading, homecoming gigs look likely to be few and far between.

It's often the job of biographers at this stage in proceedings to speculate about what comes next for their subject and to make a few educated guesses about what the future might hold. That's not required here, because Ed Sheeran knows exactly what he doing next. He's mapped it all out and has no qualms about laying it on the table for our benefit. 'This year is my year to stay relevant until the next album,' he explained to BBC Radio Manchester. 'So I've got a lot of collaborations and singles and weird musical projects coming up that are going to keep people talking and interested. Next year the new album is coming out and the year after that if I've done well in America then there's going to be a *Collaborations Part 2*, which will be a follow on from the first one but with American acts. Then I'll do another album. Then another album. Then I'll finish off with *Collaborations Part 3* which will be with all my favourite acts I've grown up with, Van Morrison and people like that.'

It's almost as if he's challenging himself to fulfil his own ambitions. He laid out his plan to record five differently themed EPs to showcase his talents and get a record deal on his own terms: it worked. Now he's laid out his plans for the next few years – he's almost saying: 'Just watch, I know I'll do it.' If he does, it will be an astonishing achievement. If he doesn't, it'll be like fuel on the fire for Sheeran's many detractors.

One of the key factors in Sheeran's success has been the way he connects with women. Ed may have been a 'spotty, chubby, ginger teenager' but very much like his hero Damien Rice, his gigs are often filled with adoring female faces. Sheeran claims he doesn't get it and that claims he is in any way a sex symbol are off the mark: 'I make poster boy music but I'm not a poster boy,' Ed told *Access Hollywood*. 'I make music that girls fall in love with but I'm not a typical teen idol.'

His fans seem to disagree. There is even a Facebook page called Dumping Your Boyfriend Because He's Not Ed Sheeran. Ten thousand people – probably all young women – already 'like' it. Interestingly, Sheeran has said he would never take advantage of his position and sleep with a fan. This seems to have the dual effect of both disappointing some fans, while making them like him even more. Inevitably, when Sheeran said this in 2012, the readers of the *NME* took great offence. 'Could he be more boring?' one wrote on the paper's website. 'I'd like to say that I'm a rock star but I'm not,' he told *Teen Vogue*. 'I'm honestly more of a relationship kind of guy. I'm a guy you could take home to meet your mum rather than a guy your mum wouldn't like.'

His 'boy next door' image also helps explain his appeal: Ed Sheeran, Mr Nice Guy. The pop star who is always nice to people and never loses his temper. 'Oh yeah, that does happen,' he told *The Guardian*, refuting the idea that he never gets angry. 'There's times where, you know, you wouldn't be in the room. I'd just be there with my cousin or something and I'd be like, for fuck's sake, this has happened, this is shit, this is shit, this is shit. And when I've got all that out, when I'm happy again, that's when I can go back to being normal Ed and happy.'

To some this says 'New Boring', but others clearly find it highly appealing. Sheeran is a man without vices – other than Twitter: 'It's my one addiction,' he told BBC Radio Manchester. 'I don't drink, I don't take drugs ... but I tweet a lot.'

Indeed, Sheeran is a man who claims to possess an addictive personality. His current 'obsession' is tattoos as he collects emblems from the places he's visited and symbols that have special meaning, like the + sign, the Snow Patrol symbol, a Lego figure, or the drawing of himself and a plane that Damien Rice drew when he was 11. Ed also has the words *festina lente* on his arm. These were words of advice he'd received from Sir Elton John after Ed had joined the veteran singer's management stable. It means 'hasten slowly' in Latin. 'I have a very addictive personality and shouldn't have got a tattoo to begin with,' he told journalist Chris Vinnicombe. 'I got one... then I got about 23. This is why I don't take drugs or anything, because I go a bit nuts with stuff. Before this it was Lego. I had a massive Lego phase and just made loads of Lego and gave it away to a charity. Before that? Yazoo, the chocolate milk drink.'

This all feeds into Sheeran's image as – to quote a *Daily Mail* headline – 'The Coyest Boy in Pop'. It might not be fashionable but he doesn't seem to care. The same goes for his choice of musical references. His constant namechecking of Damien Rice and Nizlopi have not endeared him to his record company. It's hard to imagine less 'on trend' acts to name as major influences. The degree of influence – and the debt he owes them – seems to outweigh it. Stacey Tang, marketing manager at Atlantic Records was given the task of 'figuring out the best route to market' Sheeran when he signed to the company, not the easiest of tasks. 'Even though I tear my hair out and roll my eyes when he keeps mentioning bloody Nizlopi, that's what he likes,' she told *The Guardian*. 'He's true to himself. They're not a band that I would exalt as hugely influential or particularly cool, but then I'm not Ed so it doesn't matter. I like his honesty, I like that he likes what he likes. He's not cool. Well, he's cool in that he's a cool guy, but he's not, like, a wannabe hipster. He doesn't give a shit.'

But these are the ingredients of Sheeran's success, not the reasons for it. These are harder to pin down. Perhaps some of the people who are part of Ed's story can shed some light on it? Richard Hanley, Ed's music teacher at Thomas Mills High School in Framlingham, struggles to pinpoint a specific reason for Sheeran's success, but feels it's the low-key nature of Ed the performer which marks him out. 'It's very sparse – just him and his guitar – and maybe that means there's more of a rapport between performer and audience and the audience feels more drawn,' he told me. 'The tunes are certainly catchy and people respond to them – but it's still difficult to put your finger on.'

Lizi Hanley first saw Ed perform at a school concert nearly a decade ago. 'I was trying to think how many times I'd seen him live over the years. It must be more than 20. I've seen him at small places, supporting other bands like Nizlopi, headline gigs at the Norwich Arts Centre and festivals like Latitude. I think the best gig I ever saw was just before he became really famous. It was an intimate gig at a place called The Living Room, which is literally just a room above a pub with people sitting on cushions on the floor, really chilled out. He was playing unplugged, didn't even have a mic. It was amazing. He's used things like MySpace, Facebook and YouTube really cleverly and that's the way he's got these fans he engages with all the time. That's how people of his generation and my generation find out about these things. He's always been fan-driven and considerate of his fans and you get the feeling that he's a nice guy as well. And obviously he's worked really hard. I've taken friends of mine who haven't really been into his genre of music and they've stood there and watched him and said, "Actually this guy's really talented." You can't help but want to listen to more. He spans a lot of genres too which makes him accessible to a lot of people.'

Joe Doran went to the Suffolk Youth Theatre with Ed. He believes Sheeran talks directly with his peers, bypassing older audiences who just don't get it. 'It really surprised me the way he went from nothing to where he is now. I think it's because of his age – he sings about things that relate to my generation. But if you look at a lot of music critics who aren't his age, critically + was received quite badly because it didn't resonate with people of that generation. On his album there are songs about breaking up, there's songs about drinking to get over problems. And it's because his songs are about things of substance. "The A Team" is about a prostitute addicted to cocaine. Or "You Need Me", which is about how angry he was at the music industry.'

Ed's cousin, Gordon Burns also believes Ed's success and the way he connects with people is something that is dependent on your age. 'The interesting thing about Ed is he's now huge, selling all these amounts of records, two BRIT awards and so on. The thing I find most astonishing is that you speak to most adults and say "Ed Sheeran" they don't know who you're talking about. But kids do. Two million followers on Twitter! I said to him, "You know you've knocked me off my perch as the most famous person in our extended family? Not only have you knocked me off my perch, you've smashed me off!" I thought I was doing well with 12,000 followers. The worry is that this kind of music is a phase and whether it can develop, but if anyone can adapt he can. He's switched on, he loves his music – that's what he lives for. It's astonishing to see the guy who slept on floors and played in pubs doing so well.'

Musician Gary Dunne – who taught Ed to use the looping pedal at Sheeran's 16th birthday party – finds it hard to equate Ed 'The Star' with the Ed he knows. 'When

I walk round London and I see big billboards of Ed I don't connect that Adele-style level of fame, I don't think that's the same person. When I see Ed we talk about looping and songwriting. We talk about music. I still see him as I always did. I don't think, Oh my god it's Ed Sheeran. But his success is just mind-blowing.'

Why has Ed Sheeran been so successful? This is Gary's take: 'He's a naturally gifted songwriter with a very strong pop sensibility. He's frighteningly hardworking. He's an amazing people person. He works with great people. He's incredible live. Another key thing is his web savviness – he was on that from day one. He grew up with social media, he completely got it and he still does. Talent, hard work, people skills, intelligence, great parents. What more would you want?'

Tony Moore of The Bedford, where Ed recorded his live album: 'I think it boils down to one key ingredient: the ability to absorb and understand what needs to be done to make great, successful music and be able to perform and entertain audiences. A challenge for lots of performers is the ability to look outside yourself and see what people will enjoy hearing – not just what you would enjoy to write and create. Sometimes you hit a point where what you instinctively want to do and what people want to hear coincides and dovetails perfectly. When he stands on stage, people listen. He emanates confidence and control. When he sings he has a quality in his voice which touches your heart and doesn't sound like anyone else.

'Very interestingly, he came along at a time when music

and the barriers between types of music were beginning to crumble. To mix hip hop and rap with acoustic folk music – Ed has taken elements of R&B culture and hip hop culture and acoustic folk culture and blended them like Eminem did with rap. Eminem became one of the most successful rappers in the world in a genre that he shouldn't belong. But he did it better than anyone else in a way that was more accessible. Ed's done that in his own way, introduced people to different music forms. I think it's dedication, focus. He's watched, learned and absorbed what people were doing around him and then created his own style. He's original in what he does, he's innovative in the way he does it and he didn't deviate. He just kept going. No matter how tough it was, no matter how much personal stuff he had to deal with – I know he had challenges with management companies – he just kept going. Wherever there was a sofa to crash on and an audience to play to he would go and do it. I think that marks him out from everybody else.'

Jonathan De Veaux was the man who provided Ed with his first stage on that vital first trip to America. The manager of The Savoy in Inglewood, Los Angeles is shocked when I tell him the number of tickets he has sold for his upcoming UK tour: 78,000 in the first 24 hours. 'That's crazy. That's nuts. The reason that he's selling out shows – and I believe he won your version of the Grammys – is because the guy's unbelievably talented. The same thing that everybody there sees is what we all saw at The Savoy. I'm not surprised. It happened kind of sudden, though. He became a real big star really fast. We're not really tuned into

England that much, but I had heard from some people that he was a big star. But I didn't know how big he was. I exchange some emails with him and I said, "I heard you're really big now" and he said, "It's getting kind of crazy now." He's a modest guy. He's a real humble guy – I'm happy for him.'

These are all valid, heartfelt reasons. But what about Ed himself? What does he put his success down to? What quality does he have that his 'competition' doesn't? In 2011 he was asked a question that many pop stars and musicians are asked. It's a staple of many an interview. 'Choose one word that describes you best.' In Ed Sheeran's case, the answer was telling: 'Driven,' he said. 'I guess driven is the right word.'